Recipes Menus
Prayers

for

Family Gatherings

Menus & Recipes by Carolyn Anderson

Prayers by my cousins

Marty Harris Butler

Tom Harris

Barbara Harris Youngflesh

Enjoy!

Carolyn Anderson

Recipes Menus Prayers
for Family Gatherings

Drawings by Vanessa Chow

Cover Design by Philip Kuperberg

Bible Verses from the New International Version
selected by Rosanna Anderson

Type Georgia

DINNER TABLE BOOKS
164 Mason Street, Greenwich, CT 06830
DinnerTableBooks.com
Carolyn@GreenwichLiving.net

Contents

About This Cookbook

Recipes Menus Prayers

Family Meals with Thanks to God

I remember a Christmas Eve when I wanted a special prayer for the family gathering. The kitchen was bubbling with our family's heirloom recipes. I knew I had prepared a special meal, but I wasn't gifted with the words to spontaneously create a prayer that captured the feelings in my heart. I looked through my devotional books and found one that I could use, even though it wasn't just right for this occasion.

How I wished my cousins and daughter-in-law, all gifted with words of prayer, were with me that Christmas Eve! My cousins and daughter-in-law, who live in Indiana, New Jersey and Texas, have joined me in writing this book. They are also superb cooks. They have generously shared prayers and recipes with me.

We want to share our favorite foods and prayers with you.

We hope you enjoy this book.

May God bless you,

Carolyn, Marty, Barbara, Tom, and Rosanna

Anniversary

Prayer at an Anniversary Dinner

Dear Heavenly Father,

We are joined in a circle of love, celebrating the devotion this couple has shown each other. Thank you that "we love because you first loved us." Your love for us is unending. May we show the same consistency in our love for one another. Help us to always remember the gift of forgiveness you have given us and to be willing to share that same kindness with others. Bless this precious couple and help them to grow from mistakes they have made and to practice the ABC's of marriage: to Adore, to Banter with, and to Cherish each other. Keep laughter and love alive in each of them. May their love grow stronger each day because it rests on your Word and on your kind of love. Remind us all to be loyal in our prayers of praise to you always. We love you and pray in your gracious name. Amen.

Prayer by Marty Harris Butler

Bible Verse

Love must be sincere. Hate what is evil; cling to what is good. Be devoted to one another in brotherly love. Honor one another above yourselves. Never be lacking in zeal, but keep your spiritual fervor, serving the Lord. Be joyful in hope, patient in affliction, faithful in prayer. Share with God's people who are in need. Practice hospitality. (Romans 12:9-13)

Menu

Pepper-Crusted Steak
Sweet Potatoes with Orange and Cinnamon
Garden Coleslaw
Illena's Butterhorns
Raspberry Mousse

Pepper-Crusted Steak

How much pepper to press into the steak is a matter of taste. Happiness for me is an abundance. When you ask guests, Rare, medium or well? You might want to ask, How much pepper?

Ingredients

6 steaks (club steak or strip steak) each about 4 to 6 ounces and about ¾ inch thick

¼ cup whole black peppercorns

¼ teaspoon salt

2 tablespoons peanut oil

Ingredients for the Sauce

1 tablespoon whole black peppercorns

2 tablespoons butter

1 tablespoon flour

2 tablespoons scallions, finely minced

¾ cup cognac

2 cups heavy cream

⅓ cup buttermilk

drippings from the warming pan

Pepper-Crusted Steak

Directions for Preparing the Steak

Preheat oven to 150 degrees.

1. Trim fat from the meat.

2. Sprinkle salt on both sides of the steak.

3. Crush peppercorns by placing them in a zip lock bag and pound with a blunt instrument until crushed. Sprinkle crushed peppercorns on one side of each piece of meat. Use a rolling pin to press the peppercorns into the meat.

4. Heat peanut oil in a large skillet on medium-high heat.

5. Place steaks in skillet with the pepper side up.

6. Cook steaks to your taste. For medium steaks fry the non-pepper side for 6 minutes and the pepper side for 3 minutes.

7. Remove steaks to an ovenproof platter and keep warm in a 150-degree oven. Cooking will continue while in the warming oven, so do not leave them in the oven for more than 20 minutes.

Directions for the Sauce

1. Crush peppercorns as described above.

2. Add butter, flour, crushed peppercorns, and scallions to the skillet along with steak residue. Cook, stirring, on medium heat for 1 minute.

3. Add cognac; continue cooking and stirring for 1 minute more.

4. Stir in heavy cream and buttermilk. Cook, stirring occasionally, about 5 minutes over medium-low heat until the sauce thickens slightly (sticks to the back of the spoon). Once it begins to thicken, stir constantly for about 1 minute and remove from heat.

5. Mix any drippings from the steak's warming pan into the sauce.

Makes 6 servings

Sweet Potatoes with Orange and Cinnamon

Jerry first had these many years ago when Mrs. Yancy, a sweet friend from Virginia prepared them. We were fortunate she shared the recipe with us.

Ingredients

4 medium-sized sweet potatoes

½ cup dark brown sugar

¼ teaspoon nutmeg

1 teaspoon ground cinnamon

1 teaspoon orange zest, finely minced

1 cup fresh orange juice

2 tablespoons butter, cut into small pieces

Directions

Preheat oven to 350 degrees.

1. Place the potatoes on a baking sheet and bake for 1 hour 15 minutes in a 350-degree oven. Remove, cool, and then peel.

2. Cut the peeled potatoes in half and then slit each half lengthwise.

3. In a mixing bowl, combine sugar, nutmeg, cinnamon, and orange zest. Mix well.

4. Dip each potato section into the sugar mixture, coating and pressing the mixture into the potato.

5. Pour orange juice into a 9 x 12 inch baking dish. Place the potatoes, rounded side down, in the dish.

6. Place a small pat of butter on top of each potato and bake for 30 minutes at 350 degrees.

7. Spoon the orange juice from the pan over each potato. Serve hot.

Makes 8 to 10 servings

Garden Coleslaw

Pretty and, with this light dressing, so refreshing. The recipe was given to us by a Chinese chef.

Ingredients

4 cups green cabbage, (about ½ cabbage), grated

½ cup scallions, finely chopped

2 cups carrots, peeled and grated

¼ cup parsley, finely chopped

Ingredients for the Dressing

⅓ cup rice wine vinegar

4 tablespoons sugar

4 tablespoons canola oil

1 ½ teaspoons salt

Directions

1. Mix together cabbage, scallions, carrots, and parsley.

2. Mix together the ingredients for the dressing.

3. Stir the dressing into the cabbage mixture.

4. Refrigerate for at least 1 hour before serving.

Makes 6 to 8 servings

Illena's Butterhorns

Illena Wilson's music fills the Hillisburg Church, her garden overflows onto many neighbors' tables and her baked goods are famous all over central Indiana. This recipe is perfect for company; you can prepare the dough, refrigerate it, and take it out when you're ready to use it.

Ingredients

1 package dry yeast

½ cup sugar plus 2 tablespoons sugar

1 cup lukewarm water plus 2 tablespoons lukewarm water

½ cup melted butter (plus ¼ cup melted butter used at baking time)

3 eggs, well beaten

4 ¾ cups flour

½ teaspoon salt

Directions

1. Mix together the yeast, 2 tablespoon sugar, and the 2 tablespoons of lukewarm water. Stir and let stand 5 minutes.
2. Add ½ cup sugar, ½ cup melted butter, and beaten eggs to the yeast mixture. Mix together.
3. Sift flour and salt together.
4. In the bowl of an electric mixer, combine half of the sifted flour, the yeast-egg mixture, and 1 cup lukewarm water. Beat until smooth. Then, add the rest of the flour. Mix well.
5. Place the dough in a greased bowl, cover, and refrigerate overnight.

Preheat oven to 400 degrees.

6. Two or three hours before serving time, divide the dough into 4 parts. Roll each part on a lightly floured surface into a circle about ¼ inch thick. Spread some of the ¼ cup melted butter on each circle of dough. Cut each circle into 8 wedges with a pizza cutter. Roll each wedge from the wide end to the point. Arrange on greased baking pans. Brush with remaining melted butter. Let rise two or three hours in a warm, draft free area. (See note on page 164). Bake in a 400-degree oven for 12 minutes.

   Makes 32 rolls

Raspberry Mousse

In a tiny restaurant on the Rue du Dragon in Paris, our romance began. Was it the wonderful raspberry mousse? This recipe is as close to the original as we could create. It is a must-have on our anniversaries.

Ingredients

3 cups raspberries

4 tablespoons confectioners sugar (divided)

3 eggs

¼ cup milk

1 cup heavy cream

8 whole raspberries (for the garnish)

Directions

1. Using a food processor, puree the raspberries with 3 tablespoons sugar.
2. Press the raspberries through a fine sieve to remove the seeds. Makes about 1 ¼ cups of puree.
3. Separate the eggs. Place the yolks in one bowl and the whites in another. Set egg whites aside in a cool place.
4. Beat egg yolks.
5. In a saucepan, combine 1 cup of the pureed raspberries and the milk. Cook on medium heat, stirring until it begins to simmer. Remove from heat.
6. Slowly add about ½ cup of the hot mixture to the beaten egg yolks. Mix well and return the egg yolk mixture to the sauce pan. Continue to cook, stirring vigorously on medium heat (do not let it boil) until slightly thickened, 4 to 5 minutes. Remove from heat. Place in refrigerator to cool for at least one hour.
7. Beat egg whites until soft peaks form.
8. Beat heavy cream with one tablespoon sugar until stiff peaks form.
9. Fold the egg whites and the heavy cream into the cooled raspberries.
10. Divide the mixture among individual serving bowls or parfait glasses. Just before serving, top with a raspberry.

Makes 6 to 8 servings

Chocolate Truffles

A zesty truffle for a zesty marriage. The inspiration for these truffles came from a Famous Family cooking competition in Cape May, New Jersey.

Ingredients for the Filling

½ cup condensed milk

1 cup semisweet chocolate chips (premium)

½ teaspoon coconut extract

Ingredients for the Coating

3 tablespoons unsweetened cocoa

⅛ teaspoon cayenne pepper

2 tablespoons confectioners sugar

Directions

1. In the top of a double boiler, heat condensed milk.

2. Add chocolate chips and stir until mixture is smooth.

3. Add coconut extract, mix well and remove from heat.

4. Cool in refrigerator for about 45 minutes, stirring occasionally.

5. Scoop out teaspoon-sized dollops and roll into balls on waxed paper.

6. Combine all ingredients for coating and mix well.

7. Roll chocolate balls in coating and refrigerate until ready to serve.

8. Serve at room temperature.

Makes 16 truffles

<u>Notes</u>

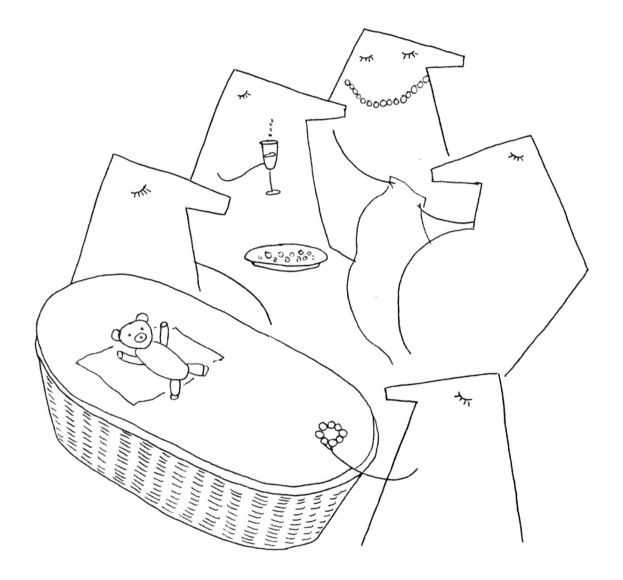

Baby Shower

Prayer at a Baby Shower

Precious Lord God,

You bring us together today to celebrate with anticipation and joy the birth of your precious child to these loving parents. May we, their family and friends, provide them wise counsel and gentle encouragement. May this child grow in faith, wisdom and strength before you. We rejoice with thanksgiving the miracle of birth and we promise to love, to walk alongside, and to be truly a circle of loving support through all of their days. In your holy name we pray. Amen.

Prayer by Barbara Harris Youngflesh

Bible Verse

For you created my inmost being; you knit me together in my mother's womb. I praise you because I am fearfully and wonderfully made; your works are wonderful, I know that full well. (Psalm 139:13-14)

Menu

> Melon Soup
> Honey Peppered Salmon
> Asparagus with Lemon Dill Sauce
> Peas in a Pod
> Broccoli Salad
> Profiteroles with Ice Cream

Melon Soup

This refreshing melon soup has a secret ingredient– a touch of pureed peach baby food. We loved the soup so much, we convinced the chef at the Field Club to share the recipe.

Ingredients

4 ½ cups of melon puree (choose your favorite melon)

1 tablespoon lime juice

2 cups vanilla yogurt

½ cup peach puree (one 8 ounce jar peach baby food)

fresh mint leaves

¼ cup sliced almonds

Directions

1. Combine the melon, lime juice, yogurt, and peach puree in a large bowl. Mix well.

2. Serve cold. Garnish with mint leaves and almond slices.

Makes 6 to 8 servings

Honey Peppered Salmon

Marinating for several hours ahead is the secret to keeping this favorite fish moist and luscious.

Ingredients

2 cups water

1 cup light brown sugar

½ teaspoon salt

2 tablespoons fresh ginger, minced

¼ tablespoon ground allspice

3 pounds salmon, skin removed

½ cup whole peppercorns (white, green, and black)

2 tablespoons honey

Directions

1. In a saucepan, mix together the water, brown sugar, salt, ginger, and allspice. Bring to a boil and then reduce heat to low. Stir on low heat until the sugar is dissolved. Remove from the heat and let the mixture cool.

2. Place the salmon in a zip lock bag. Pour the cooled mixture over the salmon and let it marinate in the refrigerator for 6 to 24 hours.

3. Soak the peppercorns in hot water for 30 minutes.

4. Drain the marinade from the salmon. Pat dry.

5. Spread honey over the fish.

6. Drain the peppercorns and press them gently into the top of the salmon.

7. Place on hot grill and cook. Be careful not to overcook as the full flavor of salmon is best when it is slightly rare.

Makes 6 to 8 servings

Asparagus with Lemon Dill Sauce

Mother's asparagus was planted along the garden fence. As a little girl I was convinced that I actually saw it growing because it shot up from the earth so fast. Choose young thin asparagus shoots. Cook briefly, remove from the pot, drizzle with dressing and serve immediately while hot and crispy.

Ingredients

2 pounds asparagus

Directions for the Asparagus

1. Snap off the end of each stalk.

2. Tie the asparagus in two bunches. Place the bunches upright in a deep cooking pot.

3. Pour about 2 inches of water in the pot. Cover and cook on high heat for 4 to 5 minutes. (Very thin shoots require a shorter cooking time.)

Ingredients for the Dressing

1 cup low fat milk
2 tablespoons cornstarch
1 egg white
4 tablespoons lemon juice
½ cup fresh dill, finely chopped
1 lemon, thinly sliced
¼ teaspoon salt

Directions for the Dressing

1. Combine the milk and cornstarch in an electric blender and blend until smooth. Pour into a pan and cook over low heat, stirring constantly until the mixture thickens. Cool.

2. Beat egg white until stiff.

3. Add lemon juice, dill, and salt to the cooled mixture. Mix well. Fold in the beaten egg white. Serve cold over asparagus. Garnish each serving with a slice of lemon.

Makes 6 to 8 servings

Peas in a Pod

Sometimes called "snow peas" or "sugar snaps," these are the peas with the thick edible sweet and juicy shells. Uncooked, they make a great snack, but when stir-fried, they make an easy side dish.

Ingredients

2 pounds snow peas

1 tablespoon sesame oil

1 tablespoon fresh ginger, minced

2 tablespoons soy sauce

Directions

1. Remove strings or stems from peas.

2. In a skillet or wok, combine the peas, oil, ginger, and soy sauce.

3. Cook, stirring constantly on medium-high heat for 4 or 5 minutes.

Makes 6 to 8 servings

Broccoli Salad

This salad is mixed with memories of gardening with my mother. We were always so happy when we discovered enough broccoli to make this salad.

Ingredients

3 cups raw broccoli flowerets, chopped into small "tiny bouquet" pieces

6 eggs, hard boiled and chopped

¾ cup pimento-stuffed olives, sliced in half

1 cup celery, finely chopped

½ cup onion, finely chopped

½ cup mayonnaise

½ teaspoon salt

Directions

1. Combine all ingredients.

2. Mix well.

3. Serve cold.

Makes 6 to 8 servings

Profiteroles with Ice Cream

Small cream puffs filled with ice cream, piled in a mound on a plate and topped with oodles of hot fudge sauce-- Oh, so delicious! The puffs filled with ice cream may be made the day before and kept in the freezer.

Ingredients

½ cup water

½ cup fat free milk

¼ teaspoon salt

½ cup margarine

1 cup flour (unbleached flour is best)

4 large eggs

vanilla ice cream (see recipe page 154)

hot fudge sauce (see recipe page 155)

Directions

Preheat oven to 425 degrees.

1. In a saucepan, combine water, milk and salt. Stirring, heat to a boil. Add margarine and continue boiling and stirring until margarine melts. Add flour all at once to the rapidly boiling mixture.
2. Stir about one minute until a ball is formed in the center of the pan. Mash the ball down against the bottom of the pan, then stir into a ball and mash down one more time. After you have reformed the ball, remove from the heat.
3. Place the ball in an electric mixer. Using the mixer, beat occasionally for about 5 minutes, so the mixture can cool to approximately 140 degrees.
4. Beat the eggs and pour into the dough. Continue to beat until well blended.
5. Drop dough by tablespoon amounts, 3 inches apart, onto a cookie sheet covered with parchment paper.
6. Bake at 425 degrees for the first 15 minutes and at 375 degrees for the remaining 5 minutes. The puffs are done when they are dry and light brown in color.
7. When the puffs are cool, cut tops off, remove insides, and fill with ice cream.
8. Just before serving, mound the puffs on each plate and cover with hot fudge.

Makes 6 to 8 servings

Barbecue

Prayer at a Barbecue

Heavenly Father,

We offer you thanks for the many blessings that have been poured out upon us. These blessings include those senses that allow us to enjoy the world you created. One of these great gifts is the ability to taste and enjoy the foods that you have provided so abundantly. You have given us taste buds that allow us to distinguish many different flavors, flavors that in so many ways give us great pleasure. As we are about to enjoy this wonderful meal of many diverse tastes, we thank you for your provision to us. We praise you for this meal in the name of Jesus Christ, our Lord and Savior. Amen.

Prayer by Tom Harris

Bible Verse

Jesus then took the loaves, gave thanks, and distributed to those who were seated as much as they wanted. He did the same with the fish. When they had all had enough to eat, he said to his disciples "Gather the pieces that are left over. Let nothing be wasted." So they gathered them and filled twelve baskets with the pieces of the five barley loaves left over by those who had eaten. (John 6:11-13)

Menu

Gazpacho
Texas Marinated Steak
Texas Barbecue Sauce
Pear Spinach Salad
Baked Beans Ora Hunt
Crusty Garlic Herb Bread
Watermelon Sherbet
Mint Iced Tea

Gazpacho

Finding a pitcher of Gazpacho in the refrigerator on a hot summer day is a welcome sight. It makes a nice beginning to a summer barbecue, and it is equally good as a refreshing snack. As soon as you have garden tomatoes, you can make this soup.

Ingredients

3 cups cucumbers, peeled, seeded, and chopped (approximately 2 cucumbers)

6 cups fresh tomatoes, peeled and roughly chopped (approximately 8 tomatoes)

¼ cup onion, peeled and chopped (approximately half of a small onion)

2 cups green peppers, seeded and chopped (approximately 1 large pepper)

2 cloves garlic, peeled and chopped

½ cup cider vinegar

1 teaspoon olive oil

¼ teaspoon cumin

¼ teaspoon paprika

⅛ teaspoon red cayenne pepper

2 teaspoons salt

1 cup croutons (as a garnish)

Directions

1. In a food processor, process tomatoes for 6 to 10 seconds and cucumbers for about 1 minute. Combine in a large bowl.

2. Blend the remaining ingredients in the food processor.

3. Mix all ingredients in a large bowl and refrigerate the mixture. Let the mixture stand for several hours so the flavors can blend.

4. Garnish each serving with croutons. Serve cold.

Makes 10 servings

Texas Marinated Steak

This is an old Anderson family formula. Try letting your steaks luxuriate in this marinade for several hours before you light the barbecue grill. You will have great tasting, tender steaks.

Steak and Marinade Ingredients

6 to 8 T-bone or sirloin steaks

4 cups water

2 cups cider vinegar

1 ½ cups Worcestershire sauce

1 ⅔ cups lemon juice (8-10 lemons)

½ cup dark brown sugar

1 teaspoon garlic salt

1 teaspoon salt

1 teaspoon cracked (or freshly ground) black pepper

8 tablespoons butter

Directions

1. In a saucepan, combine all ingredients except the butter. Bring the mixture to a boil. Lower heat and simmer for 10 minutes.

2. Add butter to the hot mixture. Stir until melted.

3. Cool the mixture to room temperature. Pour over meat and refrigerate.

4. Allow meat to marinate several hours. Turn meat over occasionally.

5. Grill over charcoal and serve with Texas Barbecue Sauce (next page).

Makes 8 cups marinade

Texas Barbecue Sauce

You will discover this Anderson family recipe makes lots of sauce. We like to make the whole Texas-sized batch and then freeze the extra for following barbecues. If you find the recipe too spicy, add another ½ cup of ketchup.

Ingredients

1 cup tomato ketchup

1 cup chili sauce

¼ cup steak sauce

2 tablespoons Worcestershire sauce

½ tablespoon soy sauce

½ cup beer

¾ cup red wine vinegar

½ cup fresh lemon juice (3 lemons)

1 tablespoon corn oil

2 tablespoons spicy brown mustard

1 teaspoon dry mustard

¾ cup dark brown sugar, firmly packed

1 tablespoon freshly ground black pepper

Directions

1. Combine all ingredients and mix thoroughly using a rotary beater.

2. Cover and refrigerate for at least 12 hours before serving.

3. Extra sauce may be frozen, ready to defrost and serve at the next barbecue.

Makes approximately 5 cups

Pear Spinach Salad

Colorful, rich in flavor and texture, this refreshing salad makes a good light lunch all by itself.

Ingredients for the Salad

8 cups fresh spinach leaves, stems removed and leaves torn into small pieces

6 slices bacon, fried crisp and broken into small pieces

3 hard-boiled eggs, chopped into medium-sized pieces

1 cup red pepper, finely chopped

2 pears, peeled, cored, and roughly chopped

Ingredients for the Dressing

½ cup olive oil

3 tablespoons red wine vinegar

2 tablespoons lemon juice

1 teaspoon prepared mustard

½ teaspoon salt

¼ teaspoon ground black pepper

Directions

1. Toss spinach, bacon, eggs, red pepper and pears together.

2. To make dressing combine olive oil, vinegar, lemon juice, mustard, salt and pepper.

3. When ready to serve coat the salad with the dressing.

Makes 6 servings

Baked Beans Ora Hunt

The original recipe came with my great- great- grandmother by covered wagon from North Carolina to Indiana. I modernized the recipe to adapt it to my taste.

Ingredients

1 pound dry great northern beans, washed and rinsed
1 tablespoon baking soda
½ teaspoon salt
½ teaspoon pepper
1 pound sliced bacon
1 tablespoon spicy brown mustard
½ cup tomato sauce
¾ cup dark brown sugar
1 tablespoon Worcestershire sauce
¾ cup finely chopped onion (1 small onion)

Directions

Preheat the oven to 300 degrees

1. In a large sauce pan, cover the beans with water and add baking soda. Boil on high heat for 3 minutes, stirring to keep foam down. Remove from heat, drain and rinse.

2. Rinse the pan and put beans back in. Cover beans with about 1 inch of water. Add salt and pepper. Add ¼ pound of bacon, each slice cut in half. Simmer on low heat until the skins break (about 30 minutes). Do not boil hard or they will go to pieces.

3. Remove the bacon strips. Put the beans and remaining water in a casserole dish with a cover. Add mustard, tomato sauce, brown sugar, and Worcestershire sauce.

4. Cut the remaining bacon into small pieces and fry until crisp. Add the chopped onion to the bacon. Continue to fry, stirring until the onions are translucent. Strain the bacon and onions to remove most of the grease. Combine the bacon and onion with the bean mixture. Mix well.

5. Cover and bake at 300 degrees for 1 hour. Remove the cover and bake at 250 degrees for 2 ½ hours. Be careful not to let the water evaporate completely. Add water if necessary to keep the beans moist.

Makes 6 to 8 servings

Crusty Garlic Herb Bread

Lots of garlic and fresh herbs mixed with butter and melting into a fresh loaf of French bread is oh- so- good!

Ingredients

1 loaf of French bread

¾ cup butter, softened to room temperature

3 or 4 garlic cloves, finely minced

2 tablespoons fresh dill, finely chopped

2 tablespoons fresh parsley, finely chopped

½ teaspoon garlic powder

Directions

1. Cut the bread into 1-inch slices, being careful not to cut through to the bottom of the loaf.

2. Cream the butter with the garlic, herbs and garlic powder.

3. Spread the butter on the slices of bread. Wrap the whole loaf in foil pinching the edges together to seal.

4. Place on the grill away from the hottest coals. Turn occasionally. Heat until warm, approximately 20 minutes.

Makes 1 loaf

Watermelon Sherbet

Expect raves when you appear with this watermelon treat! The sherbet should be piled high in the watermelon shell and sprinkled with chocolate chips for seeds. This recipe first appeared in my Complete Book of Homemade Ice Cream, *published by Saturday Review Press.*

Ingredients

8 cups melon puree

2 tablespoons unflavored gelatin

1 cup sugar

2 tablespoons fresh lemon juice

1 cup chocolate chips (for garnish)

Directions

1. Cut the watermelon in half lengthwise. Scoop out the pulp and remove the seeds. Place the empty shell in the freezer while preparing the sherbet.

2. Puree the melon pulp in a blender.

3. In a small saucepan soften the gelatin in ½ cup of the melon puree and let it stand for 5 minutes. Then heat the gelatin mixture gently until dissolved.

4. Combine all of the ingredients except the chocolate chips and churn-freeze in an ice cream machine.

5. Pile the sherbet into the frozen watermelon shell. Sprinkle with chocolate chips for seeds.

Makes 8 to 10 servings

Mint Iced Tea

Wonderful for a barbecue. If you're serving it after a tennis match or any vigorous activity, be sure to double or triple the recipe. Growing up, Jerry drank gallons of this tea at Peter's house. Thanks to Peter we have this recipe.

Ingredients

2 quarts water

6 tea bags (standard black tea)

1 large bunch of fresh mint (at least 20 sprigs)

½ cup sugar

1 cup frozen concentrate orange juice

½ cup lemon juice (2 lemons)

¼ cup pineapple juice

Directions

1. Bring water to a boil.

2. Add the tea bags and mint to the boiling water.

3. Simmer for 4 minutes. Then remove the tea bags and the mint, squeezing the water out of the mint and tea bags into the pot.

4. Add the remaining ingredients.

5. Mix well, chill and serve.

Makes 8 glasses

Adult Birthday Party

Prayer at an Adult's Birthday

Dear Heavenly Father,

We know that our days were numbered and ordered by you before we were born. Each day we have been given is a gift. We celebrate the life of _____ today. Thank you for allowing our lives to touch. May every good and precious gift be his/hers today and always. We all must learn to grow up, but help us to remember that we will always be your children. You adore us and care about our lives in ways we can't even begin to imagine. May we make the most of every day, remembering where we have been but looking forward to the days ahead. May God give us wisdom and grace for each day as it passes. Help us to live in the moment. Forgive our childish ways and lead us in the path of righteousness and truth that you would have us take. In your precious name. Amen.

Prayer by Marty Harris Butler

Bible Verses

Surely goodness and love will follow me all the days of my life, and I will dwell in the house of the Lord forever. (Psalm 23:6)

For you have been my hope, O Sovereign Lord, my confidence since my youth. From birth I have relied on you; you brought me forth from my mother's womb. I will ever praise you. (Psalm 71:5-6)

Menu

> Beef Stroganoff
> Brown and White Rice
> Corn and Beans in Nutmeg Butter
> Strawberry Spinach Salad
> Hickory Nut Cake

Beef Stroganoff

Company is coming, what should we serve? This is often our choice. It's best to prepare most of this dish the day before, to allow the beef to marinate and tenderize. Just before serving, add the sour cream. Greet your guests with a smile!

Ingredients

2 ½ pounds filet of beef

6 tablespoons butter, divided

1 tablespoon olive oil

½ cup scallions, finely chopped

2 ½ cups fresh mushrooms, thinly sliced

¾ cup white wine

2 teaspoons salt

1 teaspoon freshly ground black pepper

1 tablespoon Worcestershire sauce

1 ¾ cups sour cream

Directions

1. Trim off any fat. Cut the beef into slices ¼-inch thick. Then cut each slice into ¼-inch strips.

2. In a heavy, large saucepan, combine 4 tablespoons of butter with the olive oil and heat on medium heat, until the butter melts.

3. Add the strips of beef and sauté on medium heat until lightly browned (4 to 5 minutes). Stir continuously.

4. Remove meat from the saucepan.

5. Add the remaining butter, scallions, and mushrooms to the saucepan. Cook on medium heat for 4 minutes, stirring continuously.

6. Return the beef to the saucepan. Add wine, salt, freshly ground pepper and Worcestershire sauce. Cook, stirring occasionally, on medium heat for 5 minutes. Remove from heat. Refrigerate overnight or at least 3 hours.

7. Just before serving, add the sour cream. Cook on medium heat, stirring until well mixed and heated, being careful not to boil. Serve immediately.

Makes 6 to 8 servings

Brown and White Rice

Brown and white rice have slightly different cooking times so you will need to cook them separately. The combination is delightful and worth the effort.

Ingredients

1 cup long-grain brown rice

1 cup long-grain white rice

4 ½ cups of water, divided

2 tablespoons butter, divided

Directions

1. In a saucepan, combine brown rice with 2 ½ cups water and 1 tablespoon butter.

2. Bring to a boil and then lower to a simmer, stir with a fork, cover and cook for 40 minutes. Remove from heat.

3. In a saucepan, combine white rice with 2 cups water and 1 tablespoon butter.

4. Bring to a boil and then lower heat to a simmer, stir with a fork, cover and cook for 15 minutes. Remove from heat.

5. Combine the brown and white rice. Serve warm.

Makes 8 servings

Corn and Beans in Nutmeg Butter

Fresh corn and beans are sweetest right from the garden. Everyone who gardens knows the winter fun of reading seed catalogues - so many wonderful choices. On our farm we plant Top Crop beans and Seneca Dancer corn.

Ingredients

2 cups corn

2 cups green beans, cut into 1 inch pieces (cut off tips)

¼ teaspoon salt

¼ cup butter

¼ teaspoon nutmeg

⅛ teaspoon pepper

⅛ teaspoon sugar

Directions

1. Remove the husks and silk from the fresh corn.

2. Drop the corn into a pot of boiling water. As soon as the water returns to a boil, cover and continue to cook on high for 2 minutes.

3. Remove the corn, cool, and cut the corn kernels off the cobs.

4. In a saucepan, cover the fresh green beans with water. Add the salt. Bring to a boil, then reduce the heat to low, cover, and cook for 10 minutes. Drain the beans.

5. Melt the butter. Stir in the nutmeg, pepper and sugar.

6. Combine the corn, beans and the butter mixture. Warm the mixture gently and serve warm.

Makes 6 to 8 servings

Strawberry Spinach Salad

A gift from Cousin Marty- this salad is as pretty and delicious as a salad can be!

Ingredients for the Salad

½ cup sliced or slivered almonds

8 cups fresh spinach

2 cups strawberries, thinly sliced

Ingredients for the Dressing

¼ cup cider vinegar

½ cup apple juice

½ cup olive oil

⅓ cup sugar

2 tablespoons sesame seeds

1 teaspoon poppy seeds

2 teaspoons onions, minced

½ teaspoon Worcestershire sauce

Directions

Preheat oven to 375 degrees

1. Spread the almonds in a pie plate and bake in a 375 degree oven for 20 minutes. Open the oven occasionally to stir. Remove from oven and cool.

2. In a salad bowl, toss together the spinach, strawberries and toasted almonds.

3. To prepare the dressing, combine all of the ingredients in a blender. Blend on low speed until creamy.

4. Pour dressing over spinach mixture. Toss lightly.

Makes 8 servings

Hickory Nut Cake

My favorite cake in the whole world. We have hickory nut trees around the farmhouse. Grandmother and Mother always made sure I had this cake for my birthday - no easy task. Hickory nuts are hard to crack. You can find cracked ones online or you can substitute pecans.

Ingredients for the Three-layer Cake

3 cups of sifted cake flour

3 teaspoons baking powder

½ cup butter, softened

1 ½ cups sugar

1 teaspoon vanilla extract

1 cup cold butter milk

½ cup (4 ounces) finely chopped hickory nuts (save any whole or large pieces for garnish)

3 egg whites

Ingredients for the Icing

3 cups light brown sugar, packed

1 cup plus 2 tablespoons heavy cream

1 ½ teaspoons butter

Hickory Nut Cake

Directions for the Three-layer Cake

Preheat the oven to 375 degrees

1. Grease three 8-inch round pans very sparingly; then flour and shake out. Set aside.

2. Sift the flour before measuring for 3 cups. Add baking powder to flour and "sift and sift". (Mother sifted 6 times)

3. In the bowl of an electric mixer, combine the butter and sugar. Mix well. Add vanilla. Mix well. Then add flour and butter milk alternately in small amounts until all is used.

4. Stir nuts into the cake batter. Mix well.

5. Beat egg whites until stiff peaks form. Using a spoon, gently fold the beaten egg whites into the batter.

6. Divide the batter into the 3 pans. Smooth the batter up toward the edges, with the center slightly lower. Bake until cake is lightly browned and slightly pulls away from the edges of the pan, about 25 minutes.

7. Cool in the pans for 10 minutes, then remove and cool to room temperature before icing.

Directions for the Icing

1. In a heavy saucepan, mix together the brown sugar, cream and butter. Let sit in the pan for 15 minutes before heating.

2. Cook on medium-high heat, stirring constantly, until the mixture reaches soft-ball stage, or 240 degrees on a candy thermometer.

3. Remove from the heat and pour into a mixing bowl. Cool slightly before beating.

4. Beat vigorously until the mixture is creamy smooth and ready to spread.

5. Rapidly spread icing on the cake. Garnish with hickory nuts.

Makes 10 to 14 servings

Child's Birthday

Prayer at a Child's Birthday

Kind and Loving Father,

On this very special day, we unite our hearts in laughter and joy as we celebrate yet another birthday with this delightful child whom you have given us to nurture and love. We thank you for each day we have had with him/her, as we have grown day by day in greater love and understanding. May we be brave enough to allow him/her the freedom to explore, and even at times the freedom to fail, so that he/ she, might fully develop into the amazing and wonderful person that he/she truly is. Thank you that we each can call you Abba, Daddy, Father and know that you love us as your precious children. May we celebrate you every day as we offer our prayers today. Amen.

Prayer by Barbara Harris Youngflesh

Bible Verses

Every good and perfect gift is from above, coming down from the Father of the heavenly lights, who does not change like shifting shadows. (James 1:17)

Your eyes saw my unformed body. All the days ordained for me were written in your book before one of them came to be. (Psalm 139:16)

Menu

> All-American Spaghetti Pie
> Cheese Ball with Carrots and Celery
> Chocolate Ice Cream
> Peppermint Cupcakes
> Sports Cocktail

All-American Spaghetti Pie

Just right for picnics, and church suppers, and a sure winner at birthday parties. My aunt Mary Elizabeth, a consummate cook, shared the recipe with me long ago. It has been a favorite of my children's.

Ingredients

12 ounces spaghetti

3 tablespoons butter

4 eggs, beaten

⅔ cup Parmesan cheese, grated

2 cups cream-style cottage cheese

2 pounds ground beef

1 cup onion, finely chopped

½ cup green pepper, finely chopped

3 cups canned crushed tomatoes with juice

1 teaspoon sugar

2 teaspoons dried crushed oregano

½ teaspoon garlic salt

1 ½ cups mozzarella cheese, shredded

All-American Spaghetti Pie

Directions

Preheat the oven to 350 degrees

1. Cook spaghetti according to package instructions. Drain.

2. Stir butter into the hot spaghetti, then stir in the beaten eggs and Parmesan cheese.

3. Spread the spaghetti mixture into a greased 10 x 14 inch baking pan. Spread with cottage cheese.

4. In a skillet, combine ground beef, onions, and pepper. Cook, stirring on medium heat until the meat is lightly browned.

5. Stir the tomatoes, sugar, oregano and garlic salt into the meat mixture. Mix well and heat thoroughly.

6. Spread the meat mixture over the spaghetti.

7. Bake in a 350-degree oven for 20 minutes.

8. Sprinkle with the mozzarella cheese. Bake for 5 minutes more.

9. Serve warm.

Makes 12 servings

Cheese Ball with Carrots and Celery

Light a sparkler in the middle of the cheese ball, and suddenly carrots and celery are the hit of the party. Thanks, Cousin Marty, for giving me this recipe.

Ingredients

Two 8-ounce packages of cream cheese

½ cup crushed canned pineapple, drained

¼ cup green pepper, finely chopped

2 tablespoons scallions, finely chopped

½ teaspoon seasoned salt

1 cup pecans, finely chopped

6 stalks of celery, cut into 3-inch pieces

6 carrots, peeled, sliced, and cut into 3-inch pieces

Directions

1. In the bowl of an electric mixer, combine all of the ingredients except the pecans, carrots, and celery. Mix well. Chill and then form into a ball.

2. Coat the chilled cheese ball with pecans.

3. Serve the cheese ball with celery and carrot sticks.

Makes 12 servings

Chocolate Ice Cream

In my Complete Book of Homemade Ice Cream, *I have lots of chocolate ice cream recipes. This is my very favorite.*

Ingredients

3 cups light cream, divided

2 eggs

1 ½ teaspoons flour

8 ounces dark chocolate

¼ teaspoon salt

½ cup granulated sugar

½ teaspoon vanilla

2 cups heavy cream

Directions

1. In the top of a double boiler, heat 2 cups of the light cream.

2. Beat together eggs, flour, and the remaining cup light cream and, while stirring vigorously, add to the heated cream.

3. Cook, stirring until slightly thickened. Then add chocolate, salt and sugar. Continue cooking and stirring mixture until chocolate is melted. Cool.

4. Add vanilla and lightly whipped heavy cream.

5. Using an ice cream maker, churn-freeze.

Makes ½ gallon

Peppermint Cupcakes

Prepare the peppermint milk the night before. Party guests have fun decorating their own cupcakes so have lots of sprinkles, M & Ms and miniature marshmallows on hand.

Ingredients for the Cake

¼ cup crushed peppermint (candy canes or peppermint candies crushed in a food processor)

1 cup 2 percent milk

1 ½ cups sugar

¾ cup butter

2 ½ cups sifted cake flour

3 teaspoons baking powder

¼ teaspoon salt

6 egg whites (¾ cup egg whites)

Ingredients for the Icing

3 ¾ cups confectioners sugar

½ cup butter

4 tablespoons light cream

1 teaspoon vanilla

Peppermint Cupcakes

Directions for the Cake

1. Combine the crushed peppermint with the milk. Refrigerate and let stand for at least 4 hours: overnight is best. When ready to use, strain.

Preheat oven to 375 degrees

2. In the bowl of an electric mixer, combine the sugar and butter. Beat on medium speed for 5 minutes.

3. Sift together the flour, baking powder and salt.

4. Beating between each addition, alternately add flour and peppermint milk gradually until all combined.

5. Beat egg whites just until stiff.

6. Fold the beaten egg whites into the mixture.

7. Pour batter into 24 baking cups, filling each one three-quarters full.

8. Bake at 375 degrees for approximately 20 minutes. The cupcakes should be light brown and should spring back when touched. Cool.

9. Spread icing on the cooled cupcakes.

Directions for the Icing

1. In the bowl of an electric mixer, combine all the icing ingredients. Mix on low speed until creamy and ready to spread. (Add a little more cream if necessary)

Makes 24 cupcakes

Sports Cocktail

We discovered the most popular drink at the ski slope bar in Courchevel, France was the "Cocktail Sport." On or off the ski slopes, this is a refreshing drink.

Ingredients

8 cups orange juice

3 cups grapefruit juice

6 tablespoons pineapple juice

½ cup apricot juice

Directions

1. Mix together and serve cold

Makes 12 servings

<u>Notes</u>

Brunch

Prayer at a Brunch

Holy Gracious Father,

We thank you and we praise you for all of the many good things you have provided to us. We would ask your blessing upon the meal that we are about to partake. We thank you that your provision is always adequate and good. May you bless our time together as we enjoy this meal and bless the hands that have prepared it for us. We ask this in the precious and awesome name of Christ, our redeemer and savior. Amen.

Prayer by Tom Harris

Bible Verses

This is the day the Lord has made; let us rejoice and be glad in it. (Psalm 118:24)

Because of the Lord's great love we are not consumed, for his compassions never fail. They are new every morning; great is your faithfulness. I say to myself, "The lord is my portion; therefore I will wait for him." (Lamentations 3:22-24)

Menu

> Chocolate Pancakes
> Frances's Sour Cream Coffee Cake
> Omelets with Ham, Tomatoes and Peppers
> Amy's Sausage and Cheese Casserole
> Grits Texas Style
> Fresh Fruit Salad

Chocolate Pancakes

Fry lots of crispy bacon and have a large pitcher of maple syrup. You are in for an unforgettable treat.

Ingredients

2 cups flour

3 tablespoons sweet cocoa

1 tablespoon sugar

1 tablespoon baking powder

¼ teaspoon salt

2 eggs

1 ¼ cups milk

4 tablespoons melted butter

1 cup semi-sweet chocolate chips

Directions

1. Sift together the flour, cocoa, sugar, baking powder and salt into a mixing bowl.

2. In another bowl combine eggs, milk, and butter. Using a rotary beater, mix well.

3. Stir the milk mixture into the dry ingredients. Add the chocolate chips and mix well.

4. Spoon batter in small rounds onto a hot, greased or non-stick skillet.

5. Fry until little bubbles appear and begin to pop. Then turn each pancake to fry briefly on the other side.

Makes: 10 pancakes

Frances's Sour Cream Coffee Cake

This cake blends well with the aroma of good coffee and a hearty welcome. Frances always greeted me with a warm smile and a slice of her coffee cake.

Cake Ingredients

2 cups flour

1 teaspoon baking soda

1 teaspoon baking powder

¼ teaspoon salt

½ cup butter

1 cup sugar

2 eggs

1 cup sour cream

1 teaspoon vanilla extract

Topping Ingredients

¼ cup sugar

¼ cup walnuts, chopped

1 teaspoon cinnamon

¼ cup powdered sugar (for decoration)

Directions

Preheat oven to 350 degrees.

1. Sift together flour, baking soda, baking powder, and salt.

2. In the bowl of an electric mixer, combine butter and sugar. Beat until creamy. Add eggs one at a time. Add sour cream and vanilla. Mix well. Stir in the flour mixture.

3. Mix together the granulated sugar, walnuts, and cinnamon.

4. Put topping ingredients into a buttered 8-inch tube or Bundt pan. Cover with the batter. Bake at 350 degrees for 45 minutes. Remove from pan and sprinkle with powdered sugar

Makes 8 servings

Omelets with Ham, Tomatoes, and Peppers

This colorful garden-fresh mix of peppers, tomatoes and onions is astonishingly good with eggs, simply scrambled or tucked inside an omelet. The filling can be made in a large quantity and frozen for future use.

Ingredients for the Filling

¾ pound ham, thinly sliced, cut into strips ¼ inch by 1 inch
3 tablespoons olive oil
1 cup green bell pepper, seeded and cut into 1-inch strips (1 pepper)
1 cup red bell pepper, seeded and cut into 1-inch strips (1 pepper)
1 cup yellow bell pepper, seeded and cut into 1-inch strips (1 pepper)
¾ cup onion, thinly sliced (1 small onion)
2 cloves garlic, finely minced
3 cups red tomatoes, peeled and chopped (4 large tomatoes)

Ingredients for the Omelets

12 eggs
¼ cup parsley, finely chopped
¼ teaspoon salt
¼ teaspoon freshly ground black pepper
3 tablespoons melted butter

Directions

1. In a large skillet, fry ham strips in olive oil until the ham begins to brown. Add peppers, onions and garlic and continue to fry, stirring frequently until the peppers are soft. Add tomatoes and continue to cook, stirring for 3 or 4 minutes. Remove from heat.

2. In a bowl, combine, eggs, parsley, salt and pepper. Mix using a rotary beater.

3. For each omelet, coat a hot omelet pan with butter. Into the very hot pan, pour some of the egg mixture. Give a quick stir with a fork and then let the eggs fry for a few seconds before removing the omelet from the pan (remove when the omelet is still moist but no longer runny).

4. Spread the hot vegetable mixture over each omelet.

Makes 6 small omelets

Amy's Sausage and Cheese Casserole

For hot and spicy friends, use hot sausage - or even a touch of picante sauce may be added to this easy-to-make, easy-to-eat casserole. You can slice and eat it like pizza. Leftovers are good reheated or you may simply cut the recipe in half.

Ingredients

1 pound sausage, sliced or crumbled

½ cup green onions, thinly sliced, including green tops

3 cups grated Monterey Jack cheese

1 ¼ cup flour

1 teaspoon baking powder

½ teaspoon baking soda

1 cup milk

6 eggs

¼ teaspoon salt

¼ teaspoon pepper

Directions

Preheat oven to 350 degrees

1. Butter a 13 x 9 x 2 inch baking dish.

2. Fry sausage in a pan until lightly browned.

3. Layer the cooked sausage, onions, and cheese in the baking dish.

4. Sift together flour, baking powder, and baking soda.

5. In a mixing bowl, combine the flour mixture, milk, eggs, salt and pepper. Using a rotary beater, mix well.

6. Gently pour the flour-egg mixture over the sausage in the dish.

7. Bake at 350 degrees for 30 minutes or until lightly browned.

Makes 12 servings

Grits Texas Style

A Texas recipe from my husband's Texas roots. From his viewpoint, this dish is good on any occasion.

Ingredients

1 ½ cups grits

6 cups boiling water

1 teaspoon salt

1 pound Velveeta cheese (cut into chunks)

1 cup butter

¼ cup canned pickled jalapeño peppers, finely chopped

1 dash Tabasco sauce

4 egg whites, beaten stiff

Directions

Preheat oven to 350 degrees

1. Bring water to boil. Slowly pour in salt and grits. Stir at a high boil for 1 minute.

2. Reduce heat to low, cover, and cook for about 15 minutes, stirring occasionally. If you're using quick grits, simmer for a shorter time, usually 5 to 7 minutes.

3. Add cheese and butter to cooked grits. Stir until melted.

4. Add peppers and Tabasco sauce and let cool slightly.

5. Fold in beaten egg whites.

6. Pour into a greased 8 ½ x 13 ½ inch baking dish.

7. Bake 40 to 45 minutes at 350 degrees.

Makes 8 to 10 servings

Fresh Fruit Salad

Like a bowl of sunshine, a large bowl of fruit is always a welcome sight.

Ingredients

2 cups cantaloupe

2 cups dark seedless grapes

2 cups pineapple

1 cup blueberries

1 cup pears

1 cup oranges

½ cup kiwis

1 cup raspberries

Directions

1. Cut fruit into bite-sized pieces.

2. Mix together.

3. Save the kiwis and raspberries to sprinkle on the top.

Makes 8 to 10 servings

Christmas

Prayer at a Christmas Dinner

Dear Heavenly Father,
We know that the world we live in so often focuses on "getting" and not on "giving." Today we come in thanksgiving and gratitude that you were willing to leave heaven and come to earth to live the very same kind of life we experience. You, a crying baby, a toddler, a teenager, a young adult, and yet God! The reality of humanity is difficult to comprehend. Thinking about the tremendous sacrifice you made to give us the greatest GIFT we will ever be given - Eternal Life - humbles and amazes us. May we become like the angels, who announced what the great and joyful event your birth meant for the entire earth, and sing forth praises to you each day! Help us to be more loving and kind, to find more joy in sharing and caring, and to make our lives a GIFT to others each day. In your adoring name. Amen.

Prayer by Marty Harris Butler

Bible Verses

An angel of the Lord appeared to them and the glory of the Lord shone around them, and they were terrified. But the angel said to them, "Do not be afraid. I bring you good news of great joy that will be for all the people. Today in the town of David a Savior has been born to you; he is Christ the Lord. This will be a sign to you: You will find a baby wrapped in cloths and lying in a manger." Suddenly a great company of the heavenly host appeared with the angel, praising God and saying, "Glory to God in the highest, and on earth peace to men on whom his favor rests." (Luke 2:9-12)

Menu

Holiday Ham and Raisin Sauce	Apple Butter
Sweet Potatoes with Coconut	Lemon Curd
Brussels Sprouts with Pecans	Eggnog
Apple Walnut Salad	Pecan Pie
Gingerbread	Raisin Pie
	Mulled Cider

Holiday Ham with Raisin Sauce

Our farm's meat smokehouse was abandoned in 1945. Since then, hams on our Christmas table are all from our local grocery. Place a bowl of Caroline Newburg's hot Raisin Sauce next to the ham and hope there is some left. The next day, it is oh so good, simply poured over sliced ham in a shallow dish (some more cider may be added) and baked in a 300-degree oven for 30 minutes.

Ingredients for the Ham

8-pound ham

½ cup dark brown sugar

¼ cup spicy brown mustard

Ingredients for Raisin Sauce

¾ cup raisins

1 ¾ cups apple cider

1 tablespoon cornstarch

1 level teaspoon dry mustard

⅓ cup dark brown sugar

¼ teaspoon salt

⅛ teaspoon pepper

3 tablespoons cider vinegar

Directions for Ham

Preheat oven to 300 degrees

1. Place ham in a baking dish with the fatty side up.

2. Initial baking period: Cover ham tightly with foil. Bake at 300 degrees, 20 minutes for each pound (with an 8-pound ham, bake for an initial period of 2 hours and 20 minutes).

3. Combine the brown sugar and brown mustard, mix well.

4. At the end of the initial baking period, remove ham from the oven and score with cuts in a diamond pattern.

5. Final baking period: Coat the ham with the mixture of brown sugar and mustard. Raise the oven heat to 375 degrees and return the ham, uncovered, for 20 minutes, allowing the sugar to glaze the ham.

Directions for Raisin Sauce

1. In a saucepan combine the raisins and the cider. Simmer for 10 minutes, stirring occasionally.

2. Mix together the cornstarch, dry mustard, brown sugar, salt, and pepper.

3. Stir the sugar mixture into the raisin cider mixture. Add vinegar.

4. Cook on medium heat, stirring constantly, for 3 minutes.

Makes 8 to 10 servings

Sweet Potatoes with Coconut Topping

When this recipe came into our life, sweet potatoes topped with marshmallows lost their place on the table. Oh, the joys of growing up!

Ingredients for the Casserole

3 ½ cups cooked, mashed sweet potatoes (4 medium-sized sweet potatoes)
1 cup evaporated milk
3 eggs, slightly beaten
¼ cup butter, melted
1 teaspoon vanilla extract
½ teaspoon cinnamon
¼ teaspoon salt

Ingredients for the Topping

1 cup corn flakes, crushed
½ cup pecans, chopped
½ cup light brown sugar
½ cup flaked coconut
¼ cup butter, melted

Directions

Preheat oven to 375 degrees.

1. In the bowl of an electric mixer, mix all of the casserole ingredients.

2. Spoon the sweet potato mixture into a buttered baking dish. Bake at 375 degrees for 20 minutes.

3. While the potatoes are baking, prepare the topping by mixing together all of the topping ingredients.

4. When the potatoes have baked 20 minutes, remove from oven and spread the topping over the casserole. Return to the oven. Bake at 400 degrees for 15 minutes.

Makes 8 servings

Brussels Sprouts with Pecans

When I discovered my husband didn't like brussels sprouts, I couldn't believe it. I love them. These perky little brussels sprouts will win your heart just as they did his.

Ingredients

6 cups brussels sprouts (34 sprouts)

1 tablespoon salt

⅓ cup scallions, finely chopped

3 cups chicken or vegetable broth

¾ cup pecans, roughly chopped

⅓ cup red bell pepper, finely chopped

4 tablespoons butter

¼ cup fresh parsley, finely chopped

Directions

1. Wash and trim off the outer leaves of the brussels sprouts. (Be careful not to trim the stem ends too closely so the leaves will stay on while cooking.)

2. Place the sprouts in a bowl and cover with cold water. Add the salt to the water. Stir and let the sprouts soak in the salted water for 20 minutes. Then drain and rinse with cold water.

3. In a saucepan, combine the drained sprouts, onions and chicken or vegetable broth. Bring to a boil and then reduce heat to low and cook uncovered for 5 minutes. Cover and cook for an additional 10 minutes on low heat.

4. In a small frying pan, combine the pecans, red peppers and butter. On medium heat, stirring continually, lightly sauté the mixture (only 2 or 3 minutes).

5. Garnish the sprouts with the pecans, peppers and parsley.

Makes 8 to 10 servings

Apple Walnut Salad

This is our family version of the popular 'Waldorf Salad.' We think it's the best. Prepare the dressing in advance as it needs to be cool before being poured over the salad.

Ingredients for the Salad

6 apples, peeled, cored, and finely chopped

1 cup strawberries, sliced in quarters

1 cup celery, finely sliced

¾ cup dried cranberries

1 ½ cups walnuts, roughly chopped

1 cup dark seedless grapes, cut in half

4 bananas, peeled and finely chopped

1 teaspoon lemon juice

Ingredients for the Dressing

⅓ cup cider vinegar

½ cup sugar

1 egg, beaten

1 teaspoon butter

¾ cup heavy cream

Directions

1. In a saucepan, combine vinegar, sugar, beaten egg, and butter. Cook on medium heat, stirring vigorously, using a whisk or rotary beater until the mixture begins to simmer. Remove from heat and cool.

2. Add heavy cream to the cooled mixture. Mix well.

3. Coat the banana slices with the lemon juice. Then mix together all of the salad ingredients, reserving ½ cup walnuts for garnish.

4. Pour dressing over the salad just before serving. Garnish with nuts.

Makes 10 to 12 servings

Gingerbread with Baked Apple Butter or Lemon Curd

A taste of warm gingerbread and you will wonder why we make this delicious bread, a favorite of our ancestors, only once a year. When our family is asked to make a choice between apple butter and lemon curd to top the bread, we always end up making both to please everyone.

Ingredients for Gingerbread

½ cup butter

½ cup dark brown sugar

¾ cup milk

1 cup molasses

3 cups flour

1 ¼ tablespoons ground ginger

2 teaspoons cinnamon

½ teaspoon nutmeg

1 teaspoon baking soda

1 teaspoon cream of tartar

3 eggs, beaten

Directions for Gingerbread

Preheat oven to 350 degrees

1. In the bowl of an electric mixer, combine butter and sugar. Mix until creamy. Add the milk and molasses. Mix well.

2. Sift together the flour, ginger, cinnamon, nutmeg, baking soda, and cream of tartar. Add some of the flour mixture, then some beaten egg and continue alternating until all is combined. Mix well.

3. Pour batter into a greased 12 x 8 inch baking pan. Bake at 350 degrees for 40 to 45 minutes, until a toothpick inserted in the center comes out clean.

4. Cut into squares and serve warm, with apple butter or lemon curd.

Makes 12 to 14 servings of gingerbread

Apple Butter

Baked apple butter? "Yes," Aunt Mary Elizabeth said, "Try it and you will like it forever."

Ingredients

2 ½ cups apple sauce (see Homemade Apple Sauce, page 135)

1 ½ cups dark brown sugar

2 tablespoons cider vinegar

1 teaspoon cinnamon

⅛ teaspoon ground cloves

Directions

Preheat oven to 350 degrees

1. Mix together all of the ingredients in an ovenproof dish.
2. Bake uncovered at 350 degrees for approximately 2 ½ hours.
3. Stir the mixture every 15 minutes.
4. Remove from oven when the mixture is thick and dark brown.

Makes 2 cups

Lemon Curd

One Christmas we discovered the jar of lemon curd had been Santa's midnight snack. This is so good; you won't be able resist dipping in.

Ingredients

¾ cup sugar

2 whole eggs, lightly beaten

2 egg yolks, lightly beaten

¼ cup lemon juice

¼ cup lime juice

1 tablespoon finely grated lemon zest

1 tablespoon finely grated lime zest

½ cup butter, cut into small pieces

Directions

1. In a heavy saucepan, combine all ingredients except butter.

2. Cook on moderately low heat, whisking until smooth.

3. Add butter to the mixture and cook on very low heat, stirring until smooth and thick. (Approximately 10 minutes.)

4. Pour into glass jars, cover and refrigerate.

Makes 2 cups

Eggnog

Once you try our classic eggnog, you will pass right by the commercial varieties in the grocery store. The base can be made the day before.

Ingredients for Custard Base

½ cup superfine sugar

1½ tablespoons flour

2 eggs, beaten

2 cups light cream

Ingredients for Finished Eggnog

½ cup condensed milk

1 quart light cream

½ teaspoon vanilla extract

½ teaspoon ground cinnamon

½ teaspoon ground nutmeg

Directions for Custard Base

1. Sift the flour and sugar together.

2. Stir the flour-sugar mixture into the beaten eggs and mix well.

3. In a double boiler, heat cream.

4. Slowly add, at least, ½ cup of hot cream to the egg mixture, stirring vigorously until the eggs are hot.

5. Slowly add egg mixture back to the hot cream and cook until it thickens.

6. Remove from the heat and cool.

Directions for Finished Eggnog

1. Add condensed milk and cream to the cooled custard mixture.

2. Add vanilla, cinnamon, and nutmeg and mix well.

Makes 8 servings

Pie Crust

Pie crusts are so personal. State fair judges and magazine contests will never sort out the one and only very best. Our blue ribbon goes to Mother's thin, light, flaky crust.

Ingredients

3 cups flour, unsifted

1 cup shortening

⅛ teaspoon salt

½ cup plus 2 tablespoons ice water

Directions

1. In a bowl, combine flour, shortening, and salt. Using a fork or fingers, mix together until it has the texture of corn meal.

2. Stirring with a fork, slowly pour ice water into the flour. With your fingers form the dough into 3 balls. If the dough is too dry to form balls, add a tiny bit more water. Let the dough rest for 15 minutes.

3. On floured wax paper, roll out each ball into a circle.

4. Gently fold paper and dough in half and slip dough off the paper into a pie plate and unfold the dough.

5. Trim the overlapping edges with a knife and then crimp edges with your fingers. Using a fork, prick lots of tiny holes in the crust.

Makes 3 pie crusts

Pecan Pie

Even among all those delicious homemade pies spread on the table at church suppers, this pecan is always gone first.

Ingredients

3 eggs

½ cup dark corn syrup

½ cup light corn syrup

1 tablespoon butter

½ cup sugar

1 unbaked pie crust (see preceding recipe)

1 cup pecans, ground

½ cup whole pecans

Directions

Preheat oven to 350 degrees

1. In the bowl of an electric mixer, combine the eggs, dark and light corn syrups, butter, and sugar. Mix well.

2. Pour the mixture into the unbaked pie crust (see page 73).

3. Evenly spread the ground pecans over the pie. Using a fork, gently press pecans into the pie mixture. Decorate the pie with the whole pecans.

4. Bake at 350 degrees for 50 to 60 minutes until pie is firm (not soupy) in the middle.

Makes 1 pie

Raisin Pie

This open- crusted sour cream and raisin pie won the family contest.

Ingredients

2 eggs, beaten

2 tablespoons flour

¼ teaspoon cloves

¼ teaspoon cinnamon

¼ teaspoon nutmeg

1 ¾ cups sugar

1 ¾ cups sour cream

2 cups raisins

Directions

Preheat oven to 350 degrees.

1. In a large mixing bowl, combine all of the ingredients. Mix well.

2. Let stand for 30 minutes.

3. Pour into an un-baked pie crust (see page 73).

4. Bake for approximately 50 minutes, until the pie is firm and the crust is lightly brown.

Makes 1 pie

Mulled Cider

Tom and Gale Hartch shared their family recipe with us many years ago. A cup of this warm cider is like a good hug. Its spicy aroma tells us the holidays have arrived.

Ingredients

1 gallon cider

1 cup light brown sugar

1 tablespoon whole cloves

1 tablespoon whole allspice

8 pieces whole cinnamon (2-inch-long pieces)

2 pieces whole mace

¼ teaspoon salt

1 dash of cayenne pepper

Directions

1. In a large kettle, mix all of the ingredients. Bring mixture to a boil.

2. Cook on medium-high heat for 15 minutes.

3. Strain to remove the whole spices.

4. Serve hot.

Makes 16 to 20 cups

<u>Notes</u>

Dining Alone

Prayer when Dining Alone

Dear Lord,

On these days when the table is set only for one, may I never forget that the table before me is actually set for you, as you are with me as I eat. I have never been out of your sight, I have never been truly alone, for you are always present. You have given me this opportunity again, Lord, to pause, to think, and to praise you for the miracle of your presence and the quiet moments to simply say, thank you. You have generously provided all that I need, and I love you deeply. Bless this meal. May I be nourished to serve you wherever and however you call me. Thank you for bringing your peaceful presence to me. In Christ's holy name. Amen.

Prayer by Barbara Harris Youngflesh

Bible Verse

Yet I am always with you; you hold me by my right hand. You guide me with your counsel, and afterward you will take me into glory. Whom have I in heaven but you? And earth has nothing I desire besides you. (Psalm 73:23-25)

Menu

> Chipped Beef Gravy
> Baked Potato
> Tomato and Mozzarella Cheese
> Baked Apple with Cranberries and Walnuts

Chipped Beef Gravy

Growing up, dried beef gravy was a quick answer to - "What should we eat tonight?" A jar of beef was always in the pantry. Maybe it's the recipe's simplicity that makes it rarely appear in cookbooks or on dinner tables. This gravy is mighty good on baked potatoes, toast, biscuits, or rice. Make it with memories or discover it for the first time.

Ingredients

2 ¼ ounces dried beef (one small jar or package)

¼ cup butter

¼ cup flour

3 cups milk

Directions

1. Cut beef into small pieces, (¼ x ¼ inch) and place in a strainer. Pour boiling water over the beef to remove some of the salt.

2. In a skillet, melt butter.

3. Stir the beef into the melted butter. On medium heat, fry, stirring until the beef is lightly browned.

4. Add flour to the beef and continue stirring until flour is dissolved.

5. Add milk, a small amount at a time, stirring between each addition.

6. Stir frequently and cook on medium-low heat until mixture thickens and begins to boil. Remove from heat.

7. Serve hot and refrigerate or freeze the extra.

Makes 2 Servings

Baked Potato

The best baked potatoes with crispy skins and perfect insides are baked slowly in the regular oven. If you're in a hurry, prepare the potato in the same way, then place it on a paper towel in the microwave. Cook on high for about 10 minutes. Remove the potato, test for doneness in the same way, wrap in foil, and wait 5 minutes before serving.

Ingredients

1 large potato, Idaho or Russet

½ teaspoon canola oil

Directions

Preheat oven to 350 degrees.

1. Scrub the potato and then dry. With a sharp knife, punch holes all over the potato.

2. Rub the potato with oil.

3. Place the potato on the oven rack. Place a baking sheet or pan below the rack to catch any drippings.

4. Bake for 60 to 70 minutes. Potato is done if you can puncture it easily with a thin bladed knife and when, the potato feels soft inside when squeezed gently. (Wrap your hand in a cloth before squeezing).

5. Split the potato open just before serving

Makes 1 to 2 servings (if the potato is large, half may be enough for one serving)

Tomato and Mozzarella Salad

Always best with a freshly picked, really ripe tomato. I have trouble getting used to 'store boughten' ones that are bred to have tough skins so they can be picked by machine. Pick a "Big Boy" or any homegrown tomato and you will immediately see and taste the difference. Kathy and John Augustin's tomatoes are delicious.

Ingredients

1 large ripe red tomato

½ cup fresh mozzarella cheese diced to ¼ inch cubes (⅛ pound)

4 fresh basil leaves, finely chopped

⅛ teaspoon dried oregano

1 teaspoon olive oil

⅛ teaspoon salt

pepper to taste

Directions

1. Cut the tomato into 8 or 10 sections (petals), cutting from the bud end almost all the way to the stem end.

2. Open the petals wide on a plate. (If you like, sprinkle the petals with salt.)

3. Mix together cheese cubes, basil, oregano, olive oil, salt, and pepper.

4. Spoon this mixture in the center of the tomato.

Makes 1 serving

Baked Apple with Cranberries and Walnuts

I can't resist a dollop of vanilla ice cream on this easy-to-make dessert.

Ingredients

1 large apple

1 cup cranberry juice

1 tablespoon sugar

Ingredients for the Filling

2 tablespoons honey

2 tablespoons walnuts, chopped

2 tablespoons dried cranberries

¼ teaspoon cinnamon

Directions

Preheat the oven to 350 degrees.

1. Peel the apple and then cut in half.

2. Remove the seeds and stem from each half, leaving a cavity to hold the stuffing.

3. Place apple halves in a small baking dish.

4. Mix the filling ingredients together and fill the cavity of each apple half.

5. Mix together the cranberry juice and sugar. Pour the sweetened juice over the apples.

6. Bake uncovered for about 60 minutes, until tender. During the baking, baste occasionally with the juice in the pan.

Makes 1 serving

Easter

Prayer at an Easter Sunday Dinner

Dear Heavenly Father,

We gather today to celebrate the blessing that you have provided through your Son Jesus Christ. We could never thank you enough for that gift you've given us. Through his death on the cross and resurrection from the tomb, we are assured that our sins are forgiven and we have the hope of eternal life with you. No greater love than this has ever been shown. As we prepare to enjoy this meal together, let us always remember this greatest act of love: your giving us a pathway to you through your only Son! Bless this meal now, and may we carry Easter in our hearts throughout all days. Amen.

Prayer by Tom Harris

Bible Verse

Jesus said to her "I am the resurrection and the life. He who believes in me will live, even though he dies; and whoever lives and believes in me will never die." (John 11: 25-26)

Menu

> Spinach Soup
> Mint Jelly
> Herb-Crusted Roast Leg of Lamb
> Herb-Roasted Potatoes
> Deviled Eggs
> Golden Beet Salad
> Coconut Cake

Spinach Soup

This soup, long ago given to us by a dear friend from Finland, has the taste of spring.

Ingredients

1 pound frozen spinach

3 tablespoons flour

2 tablespoons butter

1 cup milk

2 cups vegetable broth

½ teaspoon salt

¼ teaspoon freshly ground pepper

Directions

1. Cook the spinach according to the directions on the package.

2. Place cooked spinach in a blender and blend until smooth

3. In a saucepan combine the flour and butter. Heat, stirring until butter melts.

4. Add milk and continue stirring vigorously on low heat until sauce is smooth and slightly thickened.

5. Add the milk mixture to the spinach in the blender and blend until coarsely pureed.

6. In a large saucepan, combine the spinach mixture, vegetable broth, salt, and pepper.

7. Cook on low heat for 10 minutes, stirring occasionally.

Makes 6 to 8 small servings

Mint Jelly

Mint Jelly is one of Clifford's favorites. For individual servings, pour into lemon shells that have been halved and hollowed out.

Ingredients

1 cup fresh mint leaves

1 ¼ cups water

½ cup rice vinegar

3 ½ cups sugar

2 drops green food coloring

¼ cup liquid pectin

Directions

1. Wash leaves in cold water and pat dry with paper towels.
2. Finely chop mint leaves in a food processor.
3. In a saucepan, combine water and vinegar. Stirring, bring to a boil, then remove from the heat.
4. Stir food coloring and mint into the hot mixture. Cover and let soak for 15 minutes.
5. Return the pan to high heat, add sugar and stir until dissolved.
6. When the mixture has come to a full rolling boil, quickly add the pectin.
7. Stirring constantly, return the mixture to a full rolling boil and boil for 1 minute.
8. Quickly remove from heat and strain, pressing the leaves to extract all the flavor.
9. Skim off foam and pour into a serving dish or lemon shells.
10. Skim off any remaining foam, cover and cool overnight.

Makes 3 cups

Herb-Crusted Roast Leg of Lamb

So full of flavor, lamb is the perfect Easter celebration choice.

Ingredients

Leg of lamb, approximately 4 pounds, boned and butterflied.

Ingredients for the Marinade

2 tablespoons fresh sage, finely chopped

2 tablespoons fresh rosemary (needles without stems), finely chopped

2 tablespoons fresh parsley, finely chopped

2 teaspoons dried oregano

2 cups vegetable broth

2 cups white wine

Ingredients for the Herb Crust

4 tablespoons fresh sage, finely chopped

4 tablespoons fresh rosemary (needles without stems), finely chopped

4 tablespoons fresh parsley, finely chopped

1 tablespoon dried oregano

¾ cup whole-grain bread crumbs

½ cup olive oil

½ teaspoon salt

¼ teaspoon pepper

(Note this mixture is the same one used for the Herb-Roasted Potatoes)

Directions for Preparing the Lamb

1. Combine all marinade ingredients and mix well.

2. Score lamb on both sides with diagonal cuts about 1 inch apart.

3. Pour marinade over lamb, cover and refrigerate for 6 to 12 hours, turning occasionally.

Directions for Cooking the Lamb

Preheat the oven to 475 degrees.

1. Place lamb on a rack in a roasting pan and let it reach room temperature on the counter.

2. Mix the herbs and bread crumbs for the crust in a food processor until finely chopped.

3. Combine the herb mixture with olive oil and mix well.

4. Rub the herb mixture onto the lamb on both sides and pat down firmly.

5. Roast lamb for 10 minutes at 475. Turn over after 5 minutes.

6. Lower oven temperature to 325 degrees and roast for about 30 to 60 minutes, depending upon your preference for doneness (rare, medium or well done).

7. Before removing, check the lamb's internal temperature (130 degrees for rare, 170 degrees for well done).

8. When the desired internal temperature is reached, remove the lamb from the oven, cover it with foil, and let it rest for 15 minutes before slicing.

9. Slice lengthwise.

Makes 8 to 10 servings

Herb-Roasted Potatoes

These potatoes roasted in the same herbs as the lamb are so yummy, you may want to double the recipe.

Ingredients

4 cups potatoes, peeled and cut into 1-inch cubes

Ingredients for the Herb Seasoning

4 tablespoons fresh sage, finely chopped

4 tablespoons fresh rosemary (needles without stems), finely chopped

4 tablespoons fresh parsley, finely chopped

1 tablespoon dried oregano

¾ cup whole grain bread crumbs

½ cup olive oil

½ teaspoon salt

¼ teaspoon pepper

(Note: this mixture is the same one used for the Herb-Crusted Roast Leg of Lamb)

Directions

Preheat oven to 375 degrees.

1. Mix the herbs and bread crumbs in a food processor until finely chopped.

2. Combine the herb mixture with olive oil, salt and pepper and mix well.

3. Stir potatoes into the herb mixture, making sure all the potatoes are coated.

4. Spread potatoes on a baking sheet.

5. Roast for 30 to 45 minutes or until lightly browned. Turn frequently.

Makes 6 to 8 servings

Deviled Eggs

We can't remember an Easter without Deviled Eggs, always served in our great-grandmother's special antique egg platter.

Ingredients

6 hardboiled eggs

¼ cup mayonnaise

1 teaspoon cider vinegar

1 teaspoon Dijon mustard

¼ teaspoon salt

¼ teaspoon freshly ground pepper

⅛ teaspoon paprika

Directions

1. Peel and cut the eggs in half lengthwise. Remove the yolks and place them in a bowl. Mash the yolks.

2. Add mayonnaise, vinegar, mustard, salt, and pepper to the yolks. Mix well with a fork to finely mash the ingredients.

3. Fill the egg whites with the mashed yolks. Sprinkle with paprika. Serve cold.

Makes 12 servings

Golden Beet Salad

Chopped, pretty and delicious, my favorite beet salad would have set grandmother's taste buds humming! Cook the beets ahead of time so they can cool. The dressing and garnish can be made in advance.

Ingredients for the Salad

3 cups yellow (golden) beets

¾ cup fennel, thinly sliced and chopped

½ cup parsley, finely chopped

1 cup dry roasted macadamia nuts, finely chopped

¼ cup scallions, finely chopped

Ingredients for the Dressing

¼ cup rice vinegar

½ cup olive oil

1 tablespoon Dijon mustard

¼ teaspoon salt

¼ teaspoon freshly ground pepper

Ingredients for Balsamic Reduction

1 ¼ cup balsamic vinegar

1 tablespoon sugar

Ingredients for the Garnish

4 ounces goat cheese, chopped into small pieces.

Golden Beet Salad

Directions for Balsamic Reduction

1. In a small saucepan, combine the balsamic vinegar and sugar.

2. Bring mixture to a simmer. Continue to simmer on low heat, stirring occasionally, until reduced to about ¾ cup.

3. Let mixture cool to room temperature.

Directions for Salad

1. In a cooking pot, cover beets amply with water.

2. Cook on medium-high heat until tender (approximately 45 to 60 minutes depending on their size). If a fork enters easily, the beets are ready.

3. Cool the beats then, peel, thinly slice, and cut the slices into quarters.

4. In a salad bowl, toss together cooled beets, fennel, parsley, nuts and scallions.

5. Combine the ingredients for the dressing. Mix well. Stir dressing into the salad.

6. Garnish salad by dribbling the reduction and goat cheese over the top.

Makes 8 servings

Coconut Cake

Hallelujah will sing in your heart as you eat this luscious traditional Easter cake on this joyous day! The recipe has three parts: the filling, the cake and the icing. The filling can be made the day before because it takes time to thicken.

Ingredients for the Filling

1 cup light cream

½ teaspoon real coconut extract

2 egg yolks (reserve egg whites for the cake)

2 teaspoons cornstarch

2 cups white chocolate chips (about 11 ounces)

Ingredients for the Cake

1 ½ cups sugar

¾ cup butter

1 teaspoon vanilla extract

½ teaspoon coconut extract

2 ½ cups sifted cake flour

3 teaspoons baking powder

¼ teaspoon salt

1 cup 2 percent milk

6 egg whites at room temperature (¾ cup egg whites)

½ teaspoon cream of tartar

(*Ingredients and directions for icing on page 96*)

Directions for the Filling

1. In heavy saucepan, combine cream and coconut extract. Bring to a boil, stirring occasionally. Remove from heat.

2. In a small bowl, combine egg yolks and cornstarch. Mix well.

3. Stir in 3 tablespoons of the hot cream to the egg yolk mixture.

4. Slowly pour the warm egg mixture into the hot cream, stirring vigorously until well blended.

5. Continue stirring and return to a boil. Boil for about 1 minute to allow the mixture to thicken.

6. Add white chocolate chips and continue to heat and stir until melted.

7. Cool in the refrigerator for at least 4 hours before spreading on room temperature cake layers.

Directions for the Cake

Preheat the oven to 375 degrees.

1. In the bowl of an electric mixer, combine the sugar and butter. Beat on medium speed for about 5 minutes. Add vanilla and coconut extract.

2. Sift together the flour, baking powder, and salt.

3. Beating between each addition, add the flour mixture and the milk to the creamed butter and sugar, alternating flour and milk until all is combined.

4. In a separate bowl, beat egg whites. Add cream of tartar just as soft peaks form. Stop beating when stiff peaks form. Do not overbeat.

5. Fold the beaten egg whites into the mixture (use the mixer whisk).

6. Grease and flour three 8-inch round pans, then pour in the batter.

7. Bake at 375 degrees for about 25 minutes until cake is light brown and springs back when touched in the center. Cool.

8. Remove from cake pans. Spread each inside layer with the filling.

9. Spread icing over the cake and sprinkle with shredded coconut.

Ingredients for the Coconut Cake Icing

2 egg whites

1 cup sugar

⅓ cup water

2 ½ cups packaged shredded coconut

Directions for the Icing

1. Combine egg whites, sugar, and water in a heat-proof bowl. Set the bowl over a pan of boiling water. (The bowl should not touch the water.)

2. With a hand-held electric mixer, beat on low speed until the ingredients are thoroughly incorporated and the mixture is warm to the touch.

3. Beat on high speed for about 7 minutes until stiff peaks form.

4. Pour mixture into another room temperature bowl and continue to beat at high speed for 2 minutes.

5. Spread on the cake.

6. Sprinkle the cake with shredded coconut.

Makes 10 to 14 servings of Coconut Cake

<u>Notes</u>

Engagement Party

Prayer at an Engagement Party

Dear Heavenly Father,

As these two people stand on a threshold, ready to take a step of faith that the joining of their lives will bring JOY to the other, we pray for them. May they establish good boundaries instead of building walls. Give them wisdom to make decisions based on biblical principles. Thank you for the love that they share today. May it continue to grow stronger daily. Help them to see ways to complete rather than to compete with each other. May their love never fade or come to an end. Give them many loving years together. In your special name. Amen.

Prayer by Marty Harris Butler

Bible Verse

My lover spoke and said to me "Arise, my darling, my beautiful one, and come with me. See! The winter is past; the rains are over and gone. Flowers appear on the earth; the season of singing has come, the cooing of doves is heard in our land. The fig tree forms its early fruit; the blossoming vines spread their fragrance. Arise, come, my darling; my beautiful one, come with me" (Song of Songs 2: 10-13)

Menu

> Sesame Scallops
> Honey Shrimp
> Melanie's Chicken Satay
> Peanut Coconut Dipping Sauce
> Basmati Brown Rice with Grapes
> Raspberry Lemonade
> Peach Ice Cream

Sesame Scallops

When I was growing up in Indiana, scallops were a delicacy. Mother, a classics major, couldn't resist telling the story of Aphrodite rising from the sea on a scallop shell when she made this recipe. Marinated in lime juice and frosted with sesame, these scallops are as irresistible now as they were then.

Ingredients

1 ½ pound large scallops

6 tablespoons fresh lime juice

½ cup olive oil

2 tablespoons soy sauce

¼ teaspoon ground allspice

½ cup sesame seeds

Directions

1. Pull off and discard the small (tough) muscle from the side of each scallop. Rinse, drain, and pat scallops dry.

2. Mix together the olive oil, lime juice, soy sauce and allspice. Pour over scallops.

3. Marinate for at least 4 hours in the refrigerator. (The easiest way to marinate is to use a plastic bag with a seal.)

4. Thread the scallops on skewers. Sprinkle sesame seeds on the scallops. Grill until lightly cooked.

Makes 8 to 10 servings

Honey Shrimp

When our son, Clifford, was four he heard a guest exclaim, "I love this shrimp!" In a loud voice he asked, "Can you really love a shrimp?" We think you can love this one.

Ingredients

4 tablespoons honey

½ cup lemon juice

½ cup olive oil

2 tablespoons soy sauce

3 tablespoons chopped fresh cilantro

½ teaspoon red pepper flakes

1 tablespoon paprika

1 teaspoon chili powder

2 pounds large shrimp, shelled and de-veined

Directions

1. Combine all ingredients, except shrimp, and mix thoroughly.

2. Add shrimp to the mix and marinate at least 4 hours in the refrigerator. (The easiest way to marinate is to use a plastic bag with a seal.)

3. Thread shrimp on skewers and grill until lightly cooked.

Makes 8 to 10 servings

Melanie's Chicken Satay

After a dinner party, at which Melanie served her delicious satay, she graciously shared her satay secrets. Thanks, Melanie!

Ingredients

4 large chicken breasts, boneless and without skin, cut into 1-inch cubes

Ingredients for the Marinade

1 cup whole hazelnuts or brazil nuts

3 cloves garlic, finely chopped

⅓ cup scallions, finely chopped

3 tablespoons dark brown sugar

¼ cup ground coriander

½ cup lemon juice

½ cup olive oil

½ cup soy sauce

¼ teaspoon cayenne pepper

Directions

1. In a food processor, finely grind the nuts.

2. Add remaining marinade ingredients and mix thoroughly with the nuts.

3. Add chicken to the marinade and marinate at least 4 hours in the refrigerator. (The easiest way to marinate is to use a plastic bag with a seal)

4. Thread chicken on skewers and grill until cooked.

Makes 8 to 10 servings

Peanut Coconut Dipping Sauce

This sauce goes perfectly with Melanie's Chicken Satay. It's a good dip for just about everything.

Ingredients

¾ cup cream of coconut

½ cup water

½ cup creamy peanut butter

2 tablespoons soy sauce

1 tablespoon dark brown sugar

Directions

1. In a saucepan, combine cream of coconut and water.

2. While stirring, bring to boil and then remove from heat and add the remaining ingredients.

3. Blend thoroughly.

4. Serve warm.

Makes 8 to 10 servings

Basmati Brown Rice with Grapes

Incredibly aromatic, Basmati brown rice is worth seeking. This was Granddad Anderson's favorite rice. The wonderful smell always makes us think of his kitchen.

Ingredients

2 cups brown Basmati rice

4 ½ cups water

1 tablespoon butter

3 cups white seedless grapes cut into quarters

Directions

1. In a saucepan, combine the rice, water, and butter.

2. On medium-high heat, bring to a boil. Stir with a fork, lower heat and cover with a tight fitting lid.

3. Continue to cook on low heat for 45 minutes.

4. Remove from heat. Leaving the cover on, let stand for 5 minutes.

5. Stir quartered grapes into the rice.

6. Serve warm.

Makes 8 to 10 servings

Raspberry Lemonade

This is real lemonade the way it's supposed to be. On our farm, raspberries grew wild. Growing up, I didn't know packaged lemonade existed. We always squeezed the lemons. When the raspberries were ripe, we loved this combination.

Ingredients

2 cups raspberries

6 cups water

1 cup sugar

2 cups lemon juice, freshly squeezed (10 to 12 lemons)

Directions

1. Puree the raspberries and press through a sieve to remove the seeds.

2. Add the sugar to the water, heat, and stir until the sugar is dissolved. Cool.

3. Mix together lemon juice, cooled sugar-water, and raspberry puree.

4. Serve cold.

Makes 6 to 8 servings

Peach Ice Cream

During our honeymoon, my husband, Jerry, described this delicacy of his childhood. Homemade ice cream was synonymous with the blend of ripe peaches and cream that his Texas neighbors the Taylor Dabneys served. Mrs. Dabney kindly gave this recipe to me. I firmly believe a marriage filled with lots of peach ice cream will be long lasting and happy ever after.

Ingredients

2 eggs (pasteurized)

¾ cup sugar

1 teaspoon vanilla extract

½ cup condensed milk

2 cups heavy cream

2 cups milk

2 cups fresh, very ripe peaches, peeled, pitted, and mashed

Directions

1. Beat eggs and sugar together until very creamy.

2. Add vanilla, condensed milk, heavy cream, and milk.

3. Using an ice cream maker, churn-freeze to a mush.

4. Add peaches and continue to churn-freeze until firm.

Makes ½ gallon

<u>Notes</u>

Family Reunion

Prayer at a Family Reunion

Oh, Amazing and Awesome God!

 I simply find it hard to contain my joy and laughter as I look around me and see the wonderful gifts and surprises which you continually shower upon us! I am especially delighted to be here in this great group of people today! These, Lord, are my earthly family! Their faces are so familiar and dear. You have greatly blessed us with the gift of family and one another. May we always be aware you have called us to be in unity with one another. We learn that lesson best in families. We ask your blessings upon us today. We ask that your loving presence also be with those unable to join us, but always close to us in our hearts. May we, your children, bring much joy to your heart today as we celebrate the gift of families united in fellowship and love. It is in Christ's precious name that we unite as one and say "AMEN!"

Prayer by Barbara Harris Youngflesh

Bible Verses

In love he predestined us to be adopted as his sons through Jesus Christ, in accordance with his pleasure and will to the praise of his glorious grace, which he has freely given us in the One he loves. (Ephesians 1:5-6)

For this reason I kneel before the Father, from whom his whole family in heaven and on earth derives its name. (Ephesians 3:14-15)

Menu

Indiana Ham Loaf
Favorite 50's Salad
Glazed Carrots with Fresh Mint and Peas
Scalloped Potatoes
Carrot Cake with Walnuts
Classic Popovers

Indiana Ham Loaf

Shared recipes are amazing family ties. Now in our widely scattered kitchens, the mouth-watering smell of ham loaf baking– a frequently served dish in Grandmother's Indiana farm kitchen– fills us, wherever we are, with comfort and joy. Shoups Country Market in Frankfort Indiana will ship you a frozen meat mixture for ham loaf. (765-654-5626, www.shoupscountry.com).

Ingredients for Ham Loaf

2 pounds of ground meat (50 percent ham, 25 percent pork, 25 percent beef)

2 eggs

1 cup whole-wheat bread crumbs (2 slices of bread)

¼ cup milk

Ingredients for Basting Sauce

1 tablespoon dry mustard

1 ½ cups dark brown sugar

¾ cup cider vinegar

⅓ cup water

Directions

Preheat oven to 350 degrees.

1. **Ham loaves**: Combine ground meat, bread, eggs and milk. Shape into two loaves. Pat the sides firmly to create firm loaves. Place loaves in a baking dish.

2. **Basting sauce**: In a saucepan combine mustard, brown sugar, vinegar, and water. While stirring, heat to boiling. Pour the hot basting sauce over the loaves.

3. Bake the loaves at 350 degrees for 1 hour. Every 10 minutes, baste the loaves with the sauce in the bottom of the pan.

Makes 8 servings

Favorite 50's Salad

For over fifty years, our family has referred to this as our "favorite salad." Even though gelatin salads are out of fashion, when you taste this creamy pineapple mixture, we hope it becomes one of your favorites, too.

Ingredients

1 box lime gelatin (3 ounces)

1 package cream cheese (8 ounces)

15 marshmallows

1 cup boiling water

½ cup celery, finely chopped

1 cup crushed pineapple with juice

½ cup pecans, finely chopped

Directions

1. Combine the gelatin, cream cheese, marshmallows and boiling water in a blender. Blend until smooth.

2. In a 6 x 8 x 2 inch dish, combine the gelatin mixture, celery, pineapple, and nuts.

3. Stir to spread the ingredients evenly in the dish.

4. Cover with plastic wrap and refrigerate until jelled (usually 30 to 45 minutes).

Makes 6 to 8 servings

Glazed Carrots with Fresh Mint and Peas

Mint grew wild all around our Indiana farm house. This fragrant herb found its way into many of our favorite dishes. Carrots kept cool in the outside cellar and early garden peas were shelled and frozen so we could enjoy this mixture all summer long.

Ingredients

1 ½ cups carrots, peeled and sliced into thin rounds (3 carrots)

½ teaspoon salt

6 tablespoons butter

¼ cup sugar

2 tablespoons fresh mint leaves, finely chopped

3 cups peas

½ teaspoon light brown sugar and mint leaves for garnish

Directions

1. In a saucepan, combine the sliced carrots and salt. Cover with water and bring to a boil. Lower heat and cook for 3 to 4 minutes. Drain the water from the pan.

2. Add butter, sugar, and mint to the carrots. Cook on low heat, stirring until carrots are soft and the butter is melted (2 to 3 minutes). Do not drain. Remove from heat.

3. In another saucepan cover the peas with water. Bring to a boil. Cook 1 to 2 minutes until tender yet crisp.

4. Remove from heat and drain the water from the pan.

5. Combine the peas with the carrot mixture. Garnish with brown sugar and mint leaves.

Makes 6 to 8 servings

Scalloped Potatoes

Family and guests always ask for these old-fashioned scalloped potatoes.

Ingredients

8 medium-sized potatoes

½ cup butter

3 tablespoons flour

4 cups whole milk

1 ½ cups shredded Monterey Jack cheese

2 cups shredded cheddar cheese

1 teaspoon salt

Directions

Preheat oven to 350 degrees

1. Boil potatoes for 30 to 35 minutes. Remove potatoes from the pot and drop into cold water.

2. Peel and thinly slice the potatoes.

3. In a saucepan, combine butter and flour. Heat and stir until butter is melted.

4. Slowly add milk and continue stirring on low heat until the mixture begins to thicken slightly. Remove from heat.

5. Butter a 13 x 8 ½ inch baking dish. Alternate layers of potatoes with the sauce and shredded cheese. Lightly sprinkle each layer with salt.

6. Bake at 350 degrees for 1 hour.

Makes 6 to 8 servings

Carrot Cake with Walnuts

This rich, moist, chock-full-of-good-things cake will make you a fan of carrot cake forever!

Ingredients for the Cake

2 cups flour

1 teaspoon baking soda

1 teaspoon baking powder

1 teaspoon cinnamon

¼ teaspoon salt

1 cup corn oil

1 cup sugar

1 cup dark brown sugar, firmly packed

4 eggs

2 cups carrots, finely grated (3 carrots)

¾ cup raisins

Ingredients for the Icing

8 ounce package of cream cheese

4 cups powdered sugar

½ cup butter, softened

1 teaspoon vanilla extract

1 cup chopped walnuts

Carrot Cake with Walnuts

Directions for the Cake

Preheat oven to 350 degrees.

1. Sift together the flour, soda, baking powder, cinnamon, and salt. Set aside.

2. In the bowl of an electric mixer, combine the oil and white and brown sugar. Mix well.

3. Continue to mix, adding eggs one at a time. Slowly add the flour mixture and then the carrots and raisins. Mix well.

4. Pour mixture into a 13 x 8 ½ inch greased and floured pan.

5. Bake at 350 degrees for 35 to 40 minutes. Insert toothpick in center. When it comes out clean, the cake is done.

6. Allow to cool before icing.

Directions for the Icing

1. In the bowl of the electric mixer, combine cream cheese, powdered sugar, butter, and vanilla extract.

2. Mix until creamy.

3. Spread frosting on the cooled cake. Sprinkle the cake with walnuts.

Makes 12 Servings

Classic Popovers

Easy to make and fun to eat, fresh-from-the-oven popovers are perfect for informal meals.

Ingredients

1 cup flour

1 cup whole milk

2 eggs

¼ teaspoon salt

1 tablespoon melted butter

Directions

Preheat oven to 425 degrees.

1. In a bowl, combine the ingredients. Beat with a rotary beater until mixture is smooth.

2. Grease popover or muffin pans. Fill the greased tins two-thirds full with the batter.

3. Bake at 425 degrees for 40 minutes.

4. In the last 5 minutes of baking, pierce each popover to let steam escape. Serve hot.

Makes 6 popovers

<u>Notes</u>

Family Supper

Prayer at a Family Supper

Our Father,

What a blessing it is to call you Father, for you have provided us with so many things: family, home, and friends. All the blessings that we enjoy come from you. The greatest of these is the relationship that you have given us through your Son Jesus Christ. We thank you that you have enabled our family to be together tonight to enjoy this meal. We would ask that you would bless this food that it be put to its use in our bodies. Bless our time together as we enjoy one another. This we pray in the name of your holy Son, Jesus Christ. Amen.

Prayer by Tom Harris

Bible Verses

May the favor of the Lord our God rest upon us; establish the work of our hands for us— yes, establish the work of our hands. (Psalm 90:17)

I can do everything through him who gives me strength. (Philippians 4:13)

Menu

> Texas Chicken-Fried Steak and Gravy
> Black-Eyed Peas and Rice
> Radish Salad
> Fried Peach Pies
> Jalapeño Cornbread

Texas Chicken-Fried Steak and Gravy

What better way to bring back memories of a wonderful Texas childhood than frying chicken- fried steaks? According to Jerry, our family expert, this is the way CFS should be done. We have preserved some of the original flavor of the instructions.

Ingredients for the CFS

6 pieces top round steak, thin steaks (often called braciole or sandwich steaks)

1 cup flour

1 teaspoon salt

½ teaspoon pepper

3 eggs, beaten

¼ cup milk

½ cup vegetable oil (for frying)

Ingredients for the Gravy

4 tablespoons oil (use oil from frying the steaks)

4 tablespoons flour (use any of the flour leftover after dredging the steaks)

1 ⅔ cups whole milk

¼ teaspoon salt

Directions for the CFS

1. Tenderize each piece of meat by pounding it on both sides with a meat mallet. Keep pounding until it is very thin and flattened. Don't worry if you make holes in it. You can't pound it too much!

2. Mix together the flour, salt, and pepper in a pie plate.

3. In a second pie plate, mix together the beaten eggs and ¼ cup milk.

4. Dredge each piece of steak first into the flour mixture, coating both sides, and then in the egg mixture. Dredge again in the flour mixture.

5. Heat some of the oil in a skillet. (About ¼ inch in the bottom.)

6. On medium-high heat, fry each piece of meat, turning when the down side is lightly browned.

7. When both sides are browned, remove from the skillet and drain on paper towels. Add more oil to the skillet as needed.

8. Keep the leftover flour from the dredging and the oil in the skillet for making the gravy.

Directions for the Gravy

1. Remove all but about 4 tablespoons oil from the skillet. Use a strainer so you won't lose the browned pieces from the frying of the meat.

2. Add the flour to the oil. Stir, scraping the bottom of the skillet to break loose any pieces from the frying. Mix well.

3. Cook on medium heat, stirring until the mixture is well combined.

4. Gradually, add the milk to the flour in the skillet, stirring and cooking on medium heat until it boils and thickens. Stir in salt.

Makes 6 servings

Black-Eyed Peas and Rice

Granddad Anderson cooked his peas with ham hocks. After cooking, he would remove the meat from the ham hocks, discard the fat and bones, and return the meat to the pot. Because ham hocks are not always available, this version with finely cut ham is a good runner-up.

Ingredients

1 cup dried black-eyed peas

1 pound smoked ham steak

4 cups vegetable broth

¾ cup onion, finely chopped (save ¼ cup uncooked onion for garnish)

2 cloves garlic, finely chopped

½ cup brown rice, uncooked

¼ teaspoon cracked black pepper

Directions

1. Rinse and sort peas. Combine with 4 cups of water. Soak overnight and then drain.

2. Cut the ham into tiny pieces.

3. In a cooking pot, combine the drained soaked peas, ham, vegetable broth, onion, and garlic.

4. Bring to a boil, then lower heat to a simmer, cover and cook for 40 minutes.

5. Add rice and pepper, stir and continue to cook, covered, on low heat, stirring occasionally for 30 minutes.

6. Garnish with chopped onions and serve immediately.

Makes 8 to 10 servings

Radish Salad

The year Cousin Barbara's garden overflowed with radishes, this mixture of radishes and tomatoes became a family favorite. Thanks, Barbara!

Ingredients for the Salad

2 cups radishes, very thinly sliced

1½ cups tomatoes, chopped into pieces (about ½ inch by ½ inch)

½ cup onion, very thinly sliced

2 tablespoons fresh cilantro, finely chopped

Directions for the Salad

Mix together the radishes, tomatoes, onions, and cilantro.

Ingredients for the Dressing

2 tablespoons lemon juice

2 tablespoons olive oil

½ teaspoon salt

⅛ teaspoon garlic salt

¼ teaspoon cracked black pepper

Directions for the Dressing

1. Combine the dressing ingredients in a jar with a tight lid. Shake and then pour over the salad ingredients.

2. Refrigerate the mixture for a least 1 hour before serving.

Makes 6 to 8 servings

Fried Peach Pies

Since nostalgia is a prime ingredient, making fried pies as good as Grandmother Anderson's is a challenge. This recipe is close. To grow up without having a fried pie is too sad. The Orange, Apricot, Peach Conserve in the Fourth of July Menu also makes a wonderful filling for these pies (see page 148).

Ingredients for the Crust

3 cups flour, unsifted

1 cup shortening

⅛ teaspoon salt

½ cup plus 2 tablespoons ice water

Ingredients for the Filling

3 cups peaches, peeled, sliced, and cut into small pieces (about 6 peaches), divided

2 tablespoons sugar

2 teaspoons flour

¼ teaspoon cinnamon

Ingredients for Frying and the Garnish

4 cups vegetable oil

½ cup sugar

Fried Peach Pies

Directions for the Crust

1. In a bowl, combine flour, shortening and salt. Using a fork or fingers, mix together until the mixture has the texture of corn meal.

2. Stirring with a fork, slowly pour ice water into the flour. With your fingers, form the dough into 3 balls. If the dough is too dry to form balls, add a tiny bit more water. Let dough rest for 15 minutes.

3. On floured wax paper, roll out each ball until it is very thin.

4. Cut circles approximately 4 ½ inches in diameter.

Directions for the Filling

1. In a blender, combine 1 cup peach pieces with the sugar, flour, and cinnamon. Blend to a puree.

Directions for Assembling, Frying, and Garnishing

1. Place 1 tablespoon chopped peaches in the center of each pastry circle. Top with a teaspoon of peach puree.

2. Moisten the edges of each circle with water. Fold in half. Using a fork dipped in flour, crimp the edges together.

3. Using a large, deep pan, heat 1 inch of oil to 375 degrees. Gently drop the pies into the hot oil. Fry, turning until golden brown.

4. Remove the pies from the oil and place on paper towels. While hot, sprinkle with sugar.

Makes 26 pies

Jalapeño Cornbread

A touch of hot, a touch of sweet, this bread with whole kernels of corn is an Anderson family Texas treat. Serve warm with butter.

Ingredients

½ cup flour

½ teaspoon baking soda

1 ½ teaspoons baking powder

¼ teaspoon salt

1 ½ cups corn meal

3 tablespoons butter, softened

3 tablespoons sugar

3 eggs

1 cup buttermilk

1 cup cooked corn (fresh corn cut off the cob is best)

1 tablespoon canned pickled jalapeños, finely chopped

½ cup mild cheddar cheese, grated

Directions

Preheat oven to 350 degrees.

1. Grease a 12 x 7 inch baking pan.
2. Sift together flour, baking soda, baking powder, and salt. Stir the flour mixture into the corn meal. Set aside.
3. In the bowl of an electric mixer, combine butter and sugar. Mix well.
4. Add eggs. Mix well. Then alternate adding some cornmeal mixture and then some buttermilk until all is used. Mix between additions.
5. Stir the corn and jalapeño peppers into the mixture.
6. Pour the batter into the greased pan. Sprinkle with grated cheese.
7. Bake at 350 degrees for 40 minutes.

Makes 6 to 8 servings

<u>Notes</u>

_____
_____
_____
_____
_____
_____
_____
_____
_____
_____
_____
_____
_____
_____
_____
_____
_____
_____
_____
_____
_____
_____
_____
_____
_____
_____

Father's Day

Prayer on Father's Day

Dear Heavenly Father,

Today is a special one: the day we honor our fathers. The responsibilities these men have been given are huge! Children so often look at them and attempt to mold their lives to be just like their dad's. The way they walk, talk, respond, behave: their work ethic, habits, and relationship patterns, all can be copied. Help fathers set their sights on healthy ways of living and loving. We are so thankful that you are a forgiving and faithful Father to all you have created. May your wisdom and strength be given to fathers that they might serve and honor you and that their lives would reflect Godly actions. For all the devotion and dedication they have shown to their children, we give thanks, and praise. May fathers always feel loved and appreciated. In your kind name. Amen.

Prayer by Marty Harris Butler

Bible Verse

Jesus said in the parable of the two sons*: ... So [the younger son] got up and went to his father. "But while he was still a long way off, his father saw him and was filled with compassion for him; he ran to his son and threw his arms around him and kissed him".* (Luke 15:20)

Menu

Borsch
Beef Rolls
Tod's Famous Slaw
Potato Pancakes
Applesauce
Grandpapa's Cinnamon Biscuits
Chocolate-Hazelnut Pie

Borsch

Challenged by a friend to find the best borsch, I began my quest, reading every Russian cookbook that I could find. This soup is a combination of many recipes. Feeling confident that this was a good version, I served it at a dinner party honoring a Russian ambassador. Politeness aside, he loved it and sent the recipe home to his wife. This recipe can be cut in half, but it freezes so well I always make a large batch.

Ingredients

2 pounds beef brisket (lean beef)

2 pounds beef bones

4 whole carrots, peeled

4 stalks celery

3 whole onions, peeled

½ cup parsley

1 head white cabbage, shredded (medium-sized cabbage)

6 cups beets, peeled and cut into strips ⅛ inch wide by 2 inches long (8 - 9 beets)

5 cups tomatoes, peeled and chopped (3 - 4 tomatoes)

2 tablespoons salt

½ teaspoon freshly ground black pepper

2 tablespoons red wine vinegar

1 teaspoon sugar

1 cup sour cream or plain yogurt

Borsch

Directions

1. In a large cooking pot, combine beef, beef bones and 4 quarts cold water. Bring to a boil, skimming off any froth that comes to the top.

2. Add carrots, celery, onions and parsley to the boiling beef. Cook on low heat, covered, for 3 hours.

3. Remove the bones, beef, and vegetables from the soup. Discard the bones and vegetables. Keep the beef. When it is cool enough to handle, cut into small pieces.

4. Add the shredded cabbage, beet strips, tomatoes, reserved beef pieces, salt and pepper to the soup. Cook on low heat for 1 hour.

5. Add the vinegar and sugar to the soup. Mix well. Pour into a serving dish, serve hot.

6. Serve the sour cream or yogurt in a separate dish, allowing each diner to add a dollop to the soup.

Makes 20 servings

Beef Rolls

My love affair with these hearty delicious "rouladen" (beef rolls) started many years ago while living with my German family as an AFS exchange student.

Ingredients

8 slices bacon

8 pieces top round steak (often called braciole or sandwich steaks), cut into ¼ inch or thinner slices, about 4 x 6 inches

¼ cup mustard, mild, hot, or whole grain

½ teaspoon black pepper, freshly ground

½ cup onions, peeled and finely chopped

8 slices dill pickles

¼ cup flour

bacon grease (from the frying of the bacon)

2 tablespoons vegetable oil

3 cups beef broth

dental floss, unflavored (for tying the beef rolls)

Directions

1. Fry bacon until lightly browned and almost crisp. Drain on paper towels. Reserve grease in skillet. Break each piece of bacon in half.

2. Pound each piece of beef with a meat mallet until flattened and tenderized.

3. Spread meat with a layer of mustard. Then sprinkle with black pepper and onions. Place two pieces of bacon and a pickle slice in the center of each piece of meat. Roll the beef slices into a tight cylinder. Tie each meat roll at both ends with dental floss. Make a bow so the floss can be easily removed.

4. Roll the meat rolls in flour until completely coated.

5. In a large frying pan, heat the bacon grease and vegetable oil. Place the rolls in the pan and cook on medium heat, turning the rolls frequently until brown on all sides. Place rolls in a heavy cooking pot with a tight-fitting lid. Add beef broth. Simmer on low heat, covered, for about 1 hour.

6. Remove from broth, untie and discard floss, serve hot.

Makes 8 servings

Tod's Famous Coleslaw

Multi-talented and also a creative cook, my son-in-law's coleslaw is so delicious, you will want to eat it for breakfast.

Vegetable Ingredients

4 cups green cabbage, grated (about ½ cabbage)

4 cups red cabbage, grated (about ½ cabbage)

2 cups seedless cucumber, peeled and finely diced

2 cups tomatoes, finely diced

Ingredients for the Dressing

¾ cup mayonnaise

¼ cup sour cream

3 tablespoons apple cider vinegar

2 tablespoons sugar

2 tablespoons parsley, finely chopped

2 teaspoons Dijon mustard

2 teaspoons celery seed

½ teaspoon salt

½ teaspoon black pepper

Directions

1. Grate vegetables by hand or in a food processor.
2. Combine all ingredients for the dressing. Mix well.
3. Stir the dressing into the vegetables. Mix well.
4. Refrigerate for 1 to 2 hours before serving. Serve cold.

Makes 10 servings

Potato Pancakes

Please pass the applesauce - it's so good with these pancakes. Granddad Anderson, a weekend chef, created this recipe following one of his European trips.

Ingredients

6 cups Idaho potatoes, peeled and grated (about 6 potatoes)

¾ cup onion, finely minced

1 egg, beaten

3 tablespoons applesauce (plus additional applesauce for garnish)

½ teaspoon salt

1 cup canola oil

Directions

1. Using paper towels, grab the grated potatoes and squeeze dry.

2. Mix together the potatoes, onion, egg, applesauce, salt, and pepper.

3. Heat the oil in a large heavy skillet until hot (a drop of water on the skillet will sizzle).

4. Drop ¼ cup dollops of potato mixture into the hot oil. Flatten slightly with a spoon and fry until golden brown (4 to 5 minutes on each side).

Makes 14 three-inch pancakes

Applesauce

The apple tree outside the farm house back door was the source of our applesauce. Oh so soothing, always a comfort food. Mother would serve it hot when we ate it with the main course. She loved cinnamon red hots. Stirring a few into the sauce was Mother's special touch.

Ingredients

6 cups apples, peeled, cored, and sliced (5 apples)

½ cup water

2 tablespoons sugar

1 teaspoon red hots (cinnamon candies)

Directions

1. Place apples and water in a saucepan. Bring to a simmer, stirring occasionally. Cook until apples are soft.

2. In a blender, blend the cooked apples and then return to the saucepan.

3. Add the sugar and the red hots. Cook, stirring, on medium heat until red hots dissolve.

Makes 6 to 8 servings

Grandpapa's Cinnamon Biscuits

With minor changes – such as fast-rising yeast - these are grandpapa Hunt's old fashioned biscuits we have loved for generations.

Ingredients

½ cup sugar plus 1 teaspoon to add to yeast

1 teaspoon salt

¼ cup butter

1 cup milk

2 envelopes fast-rising dry yeast (each envelope is ¼ oz)

¼ cup lukewarm water

1 egg, beaten

4 ¼ cups flour, divided

3 teaspoons cinnamon

3 tablespoons melted butter

Directions

1. In a saucepan, combine ½ cup sugar, salt, butter, and milk. Cook on medium heat, stirring occasionally, until the butter is melted. Remove from heat and pour into the bowl of an electric mixer.

2. In a separate bowl, sprinkle yeast into ¼ cup lukewarm water (100 to 120 degrees). Stir in 1 teaspoon sugar, and mix until the yeast is dissolved. Immediately add beaten egg to the yeast mixture, mix well and dump the yeast mixture into the milk mixture. Mix at medium speed for about 1 minute.

3. Sift 1 cup flour with cinnamon. Add the cinnamon-flour mixture to the milk mixture. Beat on medium speed for about 1 minute.

4. Gradually add the remaining flour while beating on low speed. Beat for 3 minutes after all flour is added.

5. Place dough on a floured surface (It will be sticky. Don't worry, just pull it out). Knead for 2 to 3 minutes.

6. Grease a crock and put the dough in the crock to rise. Brush the top of the dough with butter. Cover with a cheesecloth or thin dish towel, and set in a warm (80-90 degrees is best), draft-free spot to rise.

7. When the dough has doubled in size (about 30 to 60 minutes, depending on the temperature), roll the dough out until it is about ½ inch thick.

8. Using a cookie cutter, cut into round biscuits. Place the rounds on a greased cookie sheet, cover, and let rise in a warm, draft-free spot until doubled in size (about 30 to 60 minutes).

Preheat oven to 375 degrees.

9. Brush with melted butter and bake until lightly brown (12 to 15 minutes) in 375 degree oven.

Note: This recipe requires a warm, draft free area where the dough can rise. An easy way to do this is to use your oven. Heat the oven to 150 degrees, turn it off, then open the door slightly to bring the inside temperature down to about 90 degrees. This makes the perfect area to let your dough rise.

Makes 20 to 24 biscuits

Chocolate-Hazelnut Pie

Oh yes, this is his favorite pie!

Ingredients for the Crust

2 cups graham crackers (about 18 graham crackers)

1 cup whole hazelnuts (whole nuts are more likely to be fresh)

½ cup sugar

½ cup butter, soft (room temperature)

Ingredients for the Filling

½ cup sugar

4 tablespoons cornstarch

⅛ teaspoon salt

2 ½ cups whole milk

4 egg yolks, beaten

1 cup bittersweet chocolate chips (60 percent cacao)

½ cup Nutella (hazelnut-cocoa spread)

Ingredients for the Topping

1 cup cold heavy cream

1 tablespoon confectioners sugar

¼ cup whole hazelnuts, ground

Chocolate-Hazelnut Pie

Directions for the Crust

Preheat oven to 375 degrees

1. Using a food processor, finely crush the graham crackers and the nuts.

2. Mix together all the ingredients. Press the mixture on the bottom and sides of a 9-inch pie plate.

3. Bake at 375 degrees for about 8 minutes. Remove from the oven and cool.

Directions for the Filling

1. In a heavy saucepan, combine the sugar, cornstarch, and salt. Mix well. Slowly stir milk into the mixture.

2. On medium heat, while stirring, bring the mixture to a boil. Continue to stir and let boil for 1 minute. Remove from heat.

3. Slowly pour ½ cup of the hot mixture into the beaten egg yolks. Mix well and then stir the egg yolks into the hot mixture in the saucepan. Stirring vigorously, return mixture to a boil. Remove from heat.

4. Stir the chocolate chips and Nutella into the hot mixture. Mix well. Pour immediately into the pie crust.

5. Cool in the refrigerator for, at least, 1 hour before adding the topping.

Directions for the Topping

1. Using a rotary beater, beat together the cream and sugar until soft peaks form.

2. Spread the whipped cream on top of the cooled pie and sprinkle with ground nuts

Makes 1 pie

Fourth of July Picnic

Prayer at a Fourth of July Picnic

Holy Lord God,

On this day, we are reminded of those who came before us to this country with a dream for religious freedom. Our forbearers fought and died in the pursuit of this freedom. Our freedom has come at a high cost to us as a nation. Around the world, today, Americans will pause and remember that our citizenship is an incredible gift. May we ever be mindful of this gift. We pray for others pursuing this same freedom. Above all else, may we never forget that our greatest freedom, the freedom to seek you and to worship you in safety is the gift of your Son, our Lord and Savior, Jesus Christ, who gave his life that we might live free to choose, to believe, and to live in the light of his resurrection from all bondage of sin. It is in his name that we praise you today. Amen.

Prayer by Barbara Harris Youngflesh

Bible Verse

Live as free men, but do not use your freedom as a cover-up for evil; live as servants of God. Show proper respect to everyone: Love the brotherhood of believers, fear God, honor the king. (1 Peter 2:16-17)

Menu

Almond-Crusted Chicken Casserole
Cool Bean Medley
Hearts of Palm Salad
Pineapple, Cheddar Cheese and Pecan Salad
Mother's Buttermilk Biscuits
Orange, Apricot, Peach Conserve
Red, White and Blue Indulgence

Almond-Crusted Chicken Casserole

Forty years ago, cousin Marty Butler gave me this recipe - a star at luncheons and dinners ever since. The chicken, rice and eggs can all be cooked the night before. Reserve the chicken broth from cooked chicken. If you add more rice or chicken, add more broth. The key is to keep the mixture moist.

Ingredients for the Casserole

1 ¼ cup condensed cream of chicken soup (one 10-ounce can)

2 ½ cups diced cooked chicken

¾ cup chicken broth

1 cup mayonnaise

½ cup diced celery

2 ¼ cups cooked rice

6 eggs, hardboiled and chopped

½ teaspoon onion salt

2 teaspoons lemon juice

½ teaspoon salt

Ingredients for the Topping

1 cup sliced almonds

3 tablespoons butter, divided

2 cups crushed cornflakes

Almond-Crusted Chicken Casserole

Directions for Casserole

Preheat oven to 375 degrees.

1. In a large bowl, combine all of the casserole ingredients. Mix well.

2. Put the casserole mixture into a buttered 13 x 9 inch baking dish.

3. Spread topping on the casserole.

4. Bake at 375 degrees for 30 minutes.

Directions for Topping

1. In a frying pan, combine almonds and 1 tablespoon butter. On low heat while stirring, fry almonds until lightly browned.

2. Add the cornflakes and remaining butter. Continue to fry on low heat, stirring, until cornflakes are coated with butter.

3. Remove from heat and spread on top of the casserole.

Makes 10 to 12 servings

Cool Bean Medley

When a friend gave me this recipe many years ago, she said it should be made while singing "Back Home Again in Indiana." This is without question the best version of this popular bean dish, yet I must admit, I have never made it without humming the tune. This is a good dish to prepare the day before the picnic.

Ingredients

1 can red beans (15 ounces)

1 can white beans (15 ounces)

1 can cut green beans (15 ounces)

1 can black-eyed peas (15 ounces)

½ cup green pepper, finely minced

½ cup red pepper, finely minced

1 cup onion, finely chopped

⅓ cup corn oil

⅔ cup white vinegar

⅔ cup sugar

1 teaspoon salt

1 teaspoon cracked pepper

Directions

1. Drain and rinse all of the beans.

2. In a bowl, combine the beans, peas, peppers, and onion.

3. Mix together the corn oil, vinegar, sugar, salt, and pepper. Pour over the beans and marinate in the refrigerator for at least 4 hours. Stir occasionally.

Makes 12 servings

Hearts of Palm Salad

Served on a bed of baby spinach and sprinkled with pimientos and goat cheese, this is a festive salad for the Fourth of July. A favorite of our family year-round, it is also superb nestled in a bed of grated carrots.

Ingredients for Salad

4 cups hearts of palm, drained and sliced (two 14-ounce cans)

1 ½ cups artichoke hearts, drained and sliced (two 6-ounce cans)

8 cups baby spinach leaves

¼ cup chopped pimientos

¾ cup crumbled goat cheese

Ingredients for the Vinaigrette

4 teaspoons whole-grain mustard

8 tablespoons lemon juice

1 tablespoon white vinegar

¾ cup olive oil

½ teaspoon salt

½ teaspoon freshly ground pepper

Directions

1. Mix together the hearts of palm and artichokes. On each salad plate, arrange spinach leaves. Top with hearts of palm and artichoke hearts. Garnish with the pimientos and goat cheese.

2. Combine the mustard, lemon juice, vinegar, oil, salt, and pepper. Shake well and pour over each salad.

Makes 8 salads

Pineapple, Cheddar Cheese and Pecan Salad

This unusual salad has its roots in the Midwest. Yes, this is a salad. Try it; you'll like it. The yummy mixture goes well with many menus and will disappear in a wink.

Ingredients

1 ½ cups chunk pineapple, drained and juice reserved (14-ounce can)

2 tablespoons flour

3 tablespoons sugar

1 egg

1 cup cheddar cheese, cut into small squares

¾ cup pecans, chopped

Directions

1. In a blender, combine the pineapple juice, flour, sugar, and egg. Blend on medium speed for 30 seconds.

2. Pour the mixture into a saucepan and cook on medium-low heat, stirring until the mixture begins to thicken. Remove from the heat and cool slightly.

3. Cut each pineapple chunk in half and then combine the pineapple juice mixture, pineapple chunks, cheese, and pecans.

4. Serve cold.

Makes 6 servings

Mother's Buttermilk Biscuits

A common bread in American cookery, these biscuits are reliable and one of the best. Mother's instructions were simple. "Beat with spoon, roll or pat, cut, bake in hot oven. Serve with homemade conserve."

Ingredients

2 cups flour

2 ½ teaspoons baking powder

¼ teaspoon salt

½ cup butter

¾ cup buttermilk plus 2 tablespoons buttermilk

Directions

Preheat oven to 425 degrees.

1. Sift together flour, baking powder, and salt.

2. Using a fork (or fingers) mix butter into the flour until the mixture is fine and crumbly.

3. Add buttermilk to the flour. "Beat with spoon."

4. "Pat" or roll with a lightly floured rolling pin on a floured surface until 1 inch thick.

5. Cut into rounds with a cookie cutter or the top of a small beverage glass (2 ¼ inches in diameter).

6. Bake on an ungreased cookie sheet at 425 degrees until lightly browned (approximately 15 minutes).

Makes 8 biscuits

Orange, Apricot, Peach Conserve

This recipe was given to my mother by Zorada Smith. It goes perfectly with Mother's Buttermilk Biscuits and makes a great filling for the Fried Peach Pies (page 124).

Ingredients

½ cup minus 1 tablespoon fresh orange juice

1 cup sugar

2 cups peaches, peeled, pitted and finely chopped

2 cups apricots, peeled, pitted and finely chopped

2 cups oranges, peeled, seeded and finely chopped

Directions

1. In a heavy cooking pan, combine orange juice and sugar.

2. Cook on medium-low heat, stirring occasionally, until it makes a sugar syrup (about 5 minutes).

3. Add chopped fruits to the orange-sugar mixture.

4. Cook on very low heat for 2 hours, stirring occasionally.

5. Put into a mason jar and refrigerate until ready to use.

Makes approximately 2 cups

Red, White and Blue Indulgence

Perfect with sparklers and fireworks. My husband does not want me to make this more than once a year because he can't help gorging himself on it.

Ingredients

1 ½ cups flour
¾ cup butter
1 ½ cups pecans, finely chopped
8 ounces cream cheese
1 cup confectioners sugar
6 cups frozen whipped topping, thawed and at room temperature
3 cups milk
2 packages instant vanilla pudding (2 ¾ ounces each)
1 can cherry pie filling (21 ounces)
1 can blueberry pie filling (21 ounces)

Directions

Preheat oven to 300 degrees.

First Layer

1. Using an electric mixer, mix together the flour, butter, and chopped pecans.

2. Using your fingers, press this mixture into the bottom of a 9 x 13 inch baking dish. Bake at 300 degrees until light brown (about 30 minutes).

Second Layer

1. Using an electric mixer, mix together cream cheese, confectioners sugar, and half of the whipped topping (3 cups). Spread over the cooled first layer.

Third Layer

1. In a saucepan, combine milk and the pudding mix. Cook on medium heat, stirring until the mixture thickens. Remove from heat, cool slightly and spread on top of the second layer.

Fourth Layer

1. Spread the remaining whipped topping over the pudding. Then spread the cherries and blueberries on top. Can you make an American Flag design?

Makes 12 servings

Graduation

Prayer at a Graduation Party

Father God,

What a joy it is to gather today to celebrate this very special occasion. You have provided an opportunity to grow in knowledge and to expand our potential. Thank you for being with us during the past few years as we have furthered our education. As we look forward to the future, help us to use our new skills to do those things that will further your kingdom on this earth. We ask that you bless the food that we are about to eat and bless our time together as we celebrate this joyous occasion. We ask for a special blessing on the graduate and our time together. This we pray in the precious name of Jesus Christ. Amen.

Prayer by Tom Harris

Bible Verse

We will shout for joy when you are victorious and will lift up our banners in the name of our God. May the Lord grant all your requests. (Psalm 20:5)

Menu

Pizzas with Many Toppings
Barefoot Vanilla Ice Cream
Hot Fudge Sauce
Caramel Popcorn

Pizza with Many Toppings

Priscilla, a friend in Park Forest, Illinois, created and shared this recipe with us. As a result, growing up, my brother Stephen and I were famous for our high school pizza parties. Spread out lots of toppings and have fun creating your own personal pizza.

Ingredients for the Crust

1 envelope active dry yeast (¼ ounce)

2 teaspoons sugar

2 ¼ cups warm water (110 degrees), divided

6 ½ cups sifted flour

2 teaspoons salt

2 teaspoons olive oil

Ingredients for the Toppings

½ cup olive oil

2 to 3 cups Parmesan cheese, grated

2 cups tomato sauce

4 cups tomatoes, thinly sliced or minced

1 pound mozzarella cheese, thinly sliced into strips

3 tablespoons minced garlic

½ cup fresh basil, finely chopped

1 tablespoon oregano, dried flakes

Optional toppings

sausage, fried and chopped into pieces

chicken, grilled and cut into strips

pepperoni

peppers (jalapeño or Bell)

pineapple

Pizza with Many Toppings

Directions

Preheat the oven to 400 degrees

1. Put yeast and sugar in a cup. Add ½ cup of the warm water (110 degrees, warm to touch but not hot). Mix well. Let stand for 5 minutes in a warm place to activate the yeast. Mixture should bubble and turn beige.

2. Sift together flour and salt.

3. In a large mixing bowl, combine half of the flour, the yeast mixture, the remaining 2 cups of warm water, and the olive oil. Using a fork, mix well until all the liquid is absorbed by the flour. Then slowly stir in the rest of the flour, making a soft dough.

4. Knead the dough on a floured board for about 8 minutes, until it is smooth and rather spongy. Add a little flour when it is sticky. To knead, firmly press the palm of your hand on the dough, turn the dough and press again. Divide the dough into 4 balls and knead them a little more. Using a rolling pin, flatten each ball until it fits into a 9-inch pie pan that has been lightly coated with olive oil. Press dough up around the edges to make the crust thick enough to keep the juices in the crust. Cover with a cloth and place in a warm, draft-free place for 15 minutes.

5. Spread a teaspoon of oil over each pizza and sprinkle with grated parmesan cheese. Cover with tomato sauce, slices of tomato, and strips of mozzarella cheese. Then sprinkle with minced garlic, chopped fresh basil, dried oregano and freshly ground pepper.

6. Add any optional toppings. Drizzle a teaspoon of olive oil over the garnished pizza.

7. Bake in a 400-degree oven for 20 to 25 minutes. Take it out of the oven when it is sizzling and brown at the edges. Serve immediately.

Note: This recipe requires a warm, draft free area where the dough can rise. An easy way to do this is to use your oven. Heat the oven to 150 degrees, turn it off, then open the door slightly to bring the inside temperature down to about 90 degrees. This makes the perfect area to let your dough rise.

Makes 4 nine-inch pizzas (each pizza serves two)

Barefoot Vanilla Ice Cream

Going barefoot was forbidden until May 1. As soon as the calendar turned, our shoes came off, and we spent many hot, barefoot days eagerly watching Grandmother as she came out of the house with a crock of this cream and poured it into the freezer for Granddad to crank.

Ingredients

2 tablespoons flour

¾ cup sugar

2 eggs, beaten

2 cups light cream

1 teaspoon vanilla extract

½ cup condensed milk

4 cups heavy cream

Directions

1. Sift together flour and sugar and then combine with eggs.

2. In a saucepan, heat light cream to a boil.

3. While stirring vigorously, slowly add the egg mixture to the hot light cream.

4. Cook, stirring, on medium heat until slightly thickened. Cool.

5. Add vanilla, condensed milk, and heavy cream to the cooled mixture.

6. Churn-freeze.

Makes ½ gallon

Hot Fudge Sauce

We like hot fudge and have tried just about every combination. This is our favorite. We hope you will like it, too. The espresso powder and vanilla enhance the chocolate flavor.

Ingredients

2 ¼ cups evaporated milk

¾ cup unsweetened cocoa powder (premium)

½ teaspoon espresso powder (item 3154 at www.BakersCatalogue.com)

3 cups semi-sweet chocolate chips (premium)

1 teaspoon vanilla extract

Directions

1. In the top of a large double boiler, heat evaporated milk.

2. Very slowly sift the cocoa and espresso powder into the mixture, allowing them to mix together completely. Stir until smooth. If you mix the powders in too rapidly, you will need to use a handheld electric mixer to smooth the mixture.

3. Add chocolate chips to the hot milk and stir until the mixture is smooth.

4. Continue to cook over boiling water for 20 minutes. Stir occasionally.

5. Stir in vanilla extract.

6. Serve hot over ice cream.

Makes topping for 8 to 10 sundaes.

Caramel Popcorn

The old Monopoly game is still on top of the china closet in the farm house dining room. Ask anyone of the five cousins about those wild and boisterous games many years ago and about the bowls of popcorn we shelled and popped, and you will hear the story of the best of times. Mother sometimes added one or two brazil nuts to the popcorn. The person to find one got a prize. This Caramel Corn is not sticky. It is perfect for munching at parties or bagging for gifts.

Ingredients

1 cup popcorn kernels (unflavored)

1 cup pecans

1 cup peanuts

½ cup corn oil

Ingredients for the Caramel Coating

1 cup margarine

2 cups light brown sugar, packed

½ cup white corn syrup

½ teaspoon cream of tartar

¼ teaspoon soda

Directions for Popping

1. If you do not have a popper, an efficient way to pop corn is on the stove.

2. In an 8 to 10 quart pot, heat corn oil on medium-high heat until it sizzles or pops when you drop a kernel into the pot. If the oil begins to smoke, turn down the heat.

3. Add the popcorn evenly, cover with a lid, and cook on medium heat.

4. Shake the pot frequently.

5. When the popping slows down, lift the pot slightly above the burner and shake the pot continuously and vigorously, until it appears there will be no more pops.

6. Pour the popped corn into a large roasting pan, being careful to remove any unpopped kernels (old maids).

7. Add the nuts to the popped corn.

Directions for Caramelizing

Preheat oven to 250 degrees

1. In a saucepan, mix the caramel coating ingredients and boil for 5 minutes while stirring.

2. Pour hot caramel mixture over the corn and nuts. Mix well.

3. Bake for 1 ½ hours.

4. Open the oven and stir about every 15 minutes.

Makes 15 servings

Mother's Day

Prayer on Mother's Day

Dear Heavenly Father,

Thank you for creating mothers! These wonderful creatures who produced, watched over, nourished, and protected us are the ones we give praise to this day. For all they have given us to help us grow, we say THANKS! You chose just the right mother for us. Help her to seek your guidance in everything she speaks, so that her life will reflect your love in ways that will allow health and happiness to grow. May she feel appreciated and respected always by those she has loved. Give her long life, confidence, wisdom, and concern for all those whose lives she impacts, and may her life be filled with faith in you! In your generous name. Amen.

Prayer by Marty Harris Butler

Bible Verses

She speaks with wisdom, and faithful instruction is on her tongue. She watches over the affairs of her household and does not eat the bread of idleness. Her children arise and call her blessed; her husband also, and he praises her: Many women do noble things, but you surpass them all. (Proverbs 31: 26-29)

I have been reminded of your sincere faith, which first lived in your grandmother, and in your mother, and, I am persuaded now lives in you also. (2 Timothy 1:5)

Menu

> Apple Curry Soup
> Rice with Fresh Herbs
> Fish Baked in White Wine
> Asenath's Country Bread
> Aunt Wilma's Angel Food Cake
> Almond Cream Sauce for Angel Food Cake

Apple Curry Soup

The recipe, once lost, is found! For years this was the soup we developed to begin dinner parties. Then one day the recipe was missing. Sharing recipes has many benefits. Thanks to a good friend who had once asked for the recipe, I again have it.

Ingredients

1 tablespoon lemon juice
5 cups apples, peeled and finely chopped (about 5 apples)
6 tablespoons butter
½ cup onion, finely chopped
2 tablespoons flour
1 teaspoon hot curry powder
4 teaspoons sugar
2 ½ cups chicken broth
1 cup coconut milk, well mixed
1 cup light cream
¼ cup coconut, shredded
fresh mint leaves

Directions

1. Pour lemon juice over the chopped apples.

2. In a wide soup pot, melt the butter. Add the onions and cook, stirring, until translucent. Add the apples and continue to cook, stirring occasionally, on low heat for about 10 minutes.

3. Mix together the flour, curry powder, and sugar. Sprinkle over the mixture in the pot. Continue cooking and stirring for 3 minutes.

4. Add the chicken broth. Cook, stirring occasionally, at a low simmer for 30 minutes.

5. Add the coconut milk and light cream. Heat until the whole mixture is hot. Do not boil.

6. Garnish each serving with coconut and mint leaves.

Makes 6 to 8 servings

Rice with Fresh Herbs

Mother's herb garden was always an inspiration. With the addition of a few snippets of parsley, chives, and dill, plain rice turns into a festive dish.

Ingredients

2 cups rice

4 cups water

½ teaspoon salt

1 tablespoon butter

2 tablespoons parsley, finely chopped

2 tablespoons chives, finely chopped

2 tablespoons dill, finely chopped

Directions

1. In a saucepan, combine rice and water. On medium-high heat, bring to a boil. Add the salt and butter. Stir with a fork.

2. Reduce heat to low, cover pan with a tight-fitting lid, and cook for 14 minutes.

3. Remove from heat. Stir in the herbs. Mix well. Serve hot.

Makes 6 to 8 Servings

Fish Baked in White Wine

Mother's Day, how dear to my heart! I have so many memories of Mother in the garden, in the kitchen and at the family table. The greatest gift I can now receive is the presence of my grown-up children with their families at our table.

Ingredients

¼ cup olive oil

1 ½ cups canned crushed tomatoes

3 cups fresh tomatoes, thinly sliced

1 cup green pepper, diced

2 cups onions, thinly sliced

½ teaspoon salt

1 ¾ pounds cod, cut in pieces approximately 1 x 2 inches

1 tablespoon garlic, finely minced

24 Greek olives, pitted

2 cups potatoes, parboiled, peeled, and thinly sliced

1 ½ cups white wine

½ tablespoon black pepper, coarsely ground

24 grape tomatoes

Fish Baked in White Wine

Directions

Preheat oven to 325 degrees.

1. Using a tablespoon of the oil, coat the bottom and sides of a 13 x 9 x 2 inch baking dish.

2. Layer the crushed tomatoes, then tomato slices, green peppers and onions in the dish, lightly salting each layer.

3. Cover with a layer of fish.

4. Sprinkle garlic and olives over the fish.

5. Cover the fish with the potatoes.

6. Pour the white wine and remaining olive oil over the layers. Sprinkle with black pepper and place the grape tomatoes evenly over the top.

7. Bake uncovered at 325 degrees for approximately 1 hour, until the potatoes are lightly browned.

Makes 6 to 8 large servings

Asenath's Country Bread

From Great-grandmother Asenath Bales Carter Osborn, who died in 1899, we have some family treasures-a family Bible, a precious doll and doll quilt, and recipes. Through the years, we've made changes to this country bread, yet we still call it Asenath's.

Ingredients

2 cups milk

½ cup yellow cornmeal

½ teaspoon salt

¾ cup dark molasses

3 tablespoons butter (room temperature)

1 teaspoon ground allspice

¼ cup dark brown sugar, packed

1 cup dried currants

⅓ cup warm water

2 packages dry yeast

5 ¼ cups sifted flour

Note: This recipe requires a warm, draft free area where the dough can rise. An easy way to do this is to use your oven. Heat the oven to 150 degrees, turn it off, then open the door slightly to bring the inside temperature down to about 90 degrees. This makes the perfect area to let your dough rise.

Asenath's Country Bread

Directions

1. Combine milk, cornmeal, and salt in a sauce pan. Bring to a boil, stirring constantly, then reduce heat to low and cook for 5 minutes stirring occasionally.

2. Place the cornmeal mixture in the bowl of an electric mixer and mix on medium speed for 2 minutes to cool it.

3. Add molasses, butter, allspice, currants and sugar. Mix on low speed for 1 more minute.

4. Thoroughly mix the yeast into the warm water (about 110 degrees). Then add to the cornmeal mixture. Mix on low speed for another minute.

5. Slowly add the flour and continue to beat on low speed until thoroughly mixed and the dough becomes stiff.

6. Place the stiff dough on a floured surface. Let it rest about 5 minutes and then knead for 8 to 10 minutes until the dough is smooth and elastic.

7. Put the kneaded dough in a warm, greased bowl and rotate it so the dough is greased on the top. Cover the bowl and set in a warm, draft-free area for 40 minutes to let the dough rise.

8. Place the dough gently on a floured surface, cut into two pieces, and form into two loafs.

9. Place each loaf in a warm, greased loaf pan, cover, and set in a warm, draft-free area for 40 minutes to let it rise again.

Preheat the oven to 375 degrees.

10. Bake for 45 to 55 minutes in a 375 degree-oven. Insert toothpick in center. When it comes out clean, the bread is done.

11. Take the loaves out of the pans and place on a rack to cool.

Makes 2 loafs

Aunt Wilma's Angel Food Cake

Everyone in Clinton County, Indiana, and beyond who has tasted Aunt Wilma's Angel Food Cake will tell you it is the lightest, most delicious cake imaginable. A few hints from Aunt Wilma: be sure the egg whites are at room temperature, sift the flour before measuring, and after the batter is in the angel food cake pan, cut the mixture gently with a spatula to remove any large air pockets. She also gives the pan a solid bang before she puts it in the oven.

Ingredients

1 cup cake flour (sift before measuring)

¾ cup plus 2 tablespoons extra-fine sugar, (for step 1)

¾ cup extra-fine sugar, (for step 3)

1 ½ cups egg whites (whites from 12 eggs)

1 ½ teaspoons cream of tartar

¼ teaspoon salt

½ teaspoon almond extract

1 ½ teaspoons vanilla extract

Note: For the topping, see the Almond Cream Sauce recipe on page 168.

Aunt Wilma's Angel Food Cake

Directions

Preheat the oven to 350 degrees.

1. Sift together the flour and ¾ cup plus 2 tablespoons sugar. Sift at least 5 times. (Set aside to use in step 4.)

2. In the bowl of an electric mixer, beat egg whites on medium speed until foamy. While continuing to beat on medium speed, add the cream of tartar, salt and the almond and vanilla extracts.

3. Continue beating and gradually add ¾ cup of sugar, 2 tablespoons at a time. After the last addition of sugar, turn mixer to the highest speed and continue beating until the mixture holds stiff peaks. As soon as you note stiff peaks, stop beating. (Do not over beat.)

4. Remove the bowl from the mixer, and using a large wire whisk, gently stir by hand the sifted flour-sugar mixture (of step 1) into the egg whites. Aunt Wilma uses the mixer whisk to stir.

5. Gently spoon the batter into an ungreased angel food cake tube pan. Do not stir the mixture. Spread the batter evenly around the pan. With a spatula, make 7 or 8 straight cuts through the batter to remove any large air bubbles.

6. Bake on the lowest rack of the preheated 350 degree oven for 35 to 40 minutes, until the top springs back when pressed with a finger.

7. Remove from the oven and immediately turn upside down. Place the tube over the neck of a bottle or funnel. Leave in the pan hanging upside down until the cake cools thoroughly (about 1 ½ hours).

8. When cool, loosen the sides of the cake from the pan with a knife and remove the cake.

9. Serve with warm Almond Cream Sauce (see next page).

10. Sprinkle with slivered, toasted almonds. (To toast almonds, spread on pie plate and bake in a 350-degree oven for 20 minutes. Open the oven occasionally to stir)

Makes 12 servings

Almond Cream Sauce

Fresh Angel Food Cake with a large dollop of warm almond sauce is as ethereal as a dessert can be!

Ingredients

1 cup sugar

4 tablespoons cornstarch

¼ teaspoon salt

3 cups milk

3 egg yolks, slightly beaten

1 tablespoon butter

1 teaspoon vanilla extract

½ teaspoon almond extract

1 cup sliced almonds, toasted

Directions

1. In a saucepan, mix together sugar, cornstarch, and salt. Pour milk in slowly. While stirring, bring to a boil. Continue to boil for 1 minute. Immediately take the saucepan off of the burner.

2. Stir some of the hot mixture into the beaten egg yolks. When hot, add the egg mixture to the saucepan. Stirring constantly, boil for 1 minute and then immediately take the saucepan off of the burner.

3. Add butter, vanilla and almond extracts. Mix well.

4. Serve warm over slices of Angel Food Cake. Sprinkle with slivered toasted almonds. (To toast almonds, spread on pie plate and bake in a 350-degree oven for 20 minutes. Open oven occasionally to stir.)

Makes 12 servings

Notes

New Year's Day

Prayer on New Year's Day

Beloved Lord God,

Here we stand, on the threshold of another year. We marvel at how quickly the last one has flown, and we have reason to pause and reflect on the passage of time. Did we do what we had hoped to accomplish last year? Did we hurt or help those whom you placed in our lives? Did we offer the help we had the power to give? And especially, did we truly reflect your influence and love in our own lives and offer that same gift to others? Make us ever mindful in the time we have, that our ministry, our mission, is to glorify you, holy God, and to make your Son, our Lord Jesus, manifest to all. Give us courage for the days ahead. May we strive to be an example of forgiveness, grace, mercy, and love to all whom we encounter this new year. Amen.

Prayer by Barbara Harris Youngflesh

Bible Verse

As a prisoner for the Lord, then, I urge you to live a life worthy of the calling you have received. Be completely humble and gentle; be patient, bearing with one another in love. Make every effort to keep the unity of the Spirit through the bond of peace. (Ephesians 4:1-3)

Menu

> Hot and Sour Soup
> Lemon Tarragon Tuna
> Red Cabbage and Apples
> Black-eyed Pea Salad
> Grandmama's Biscuits
> Lemon Mint Butter
> Apple Raspberry Crisp

Hot and Sour Soup

In Chinese restaurants, if hot and sour soup is on the menu, I order it. Knowing this, my good friend Chow F. Cheng gave me his recipe.

Ingredients

2 cups pork (1 ½ pounds pork chops)

8 cups chicken broth

2 cups water plus ¼ cup water

1 tablespoon cornstarch

1 cup bamboo shoots, drained and thinly sliced

1 cup sliced canned mushrooms, drained

¼ cup dried wood ears (black fungus), soaked in water 2 hours, chopped and drained *

1 cup Szechuan (Sichuan) preserved vegetable (Chinese pickled vegetable) thinly sliced *

3 eggs, beaten

½ cup scallions, finely chopped (about 5 scallions)

3 to 4 tablespoons white vinegar

2 tablespoons sesame oil *

* Available from Chinese markets and from Amazon.com

Hot and Sour Soup

Directions

1. Cut pork away from the bone, slice the meat very thinly and cut into short strips. Keep the bones.

2. In a large cooking pot, combine pork bones, chicken broth, and 1 cup water. Bring to a boil and then simmer for 30 minutes. Remove bones from the broth and discard the bones.

3. In a mixing bowl, combine cornstarch with ¼ cup water and mix well. Add thinly sliced pork to the cornstarch and stir to coat the meat.

4. Drain and chop the wood ears.

5. Add the bamboo shoots, mushrooms and wood ears to the broth in the cooking pot.

6. Bring the broth to a boil. Then add the pork. Cover the pot and cook on medium heat until the pork is done (about 10 minutes).

7. Slowly pour the beaten eggs from a height into the pot of hot soup while stirring vigorously. Then add thinly sliced preserved vegetable and scallions and remove from the heat.

8. Add a few drops of vinegar and sesame oil to each serving.

Makes 8 to 10 servings

Lemon Tarragon Tuna

We celebrate with tuna steaks. Cook them briefly, as the flavor and texture are at their best when slightly rare.

Ingredients

6 tuna steaks (about 2 pounds)

Ingredients for the Marinade

2 tablespoons fresh tarragon

3 teaspoons fresh ginger, minced

¼ cup olive oil

2 tablespoons honey

1 tablespoon brandy

1 tablespoon soy sauce

¼ cup fresh lemon juice

Ingredients for the Lemon-Tarragon Sauce

1 cup plain whole-milk yogurt

4 teaspoons fresh tarragon, finely minced

4 teaspoons lemon zest, finely minced

4 teaspoons honey

Lemon Tarragon Tuna

Directions for the Marinade

1. Blend tarragon, ginger, and olive oil.

2. Add honey, brandy, soy sauce and lemon juice. Mix well.

Directions for the Tuna

1. Score both sides of the tuna.

2. Marinate the fish in a zip lock bag for, at least, 2 hours.

3. Drain the fish, discarding the marinade.

4. In a large skillet, heat 2 tablespoons olive oil.

5. Cook each side 3 to 3½ minutes (for medium rare) on medium heat.

Directions for the Lemon Tarragon Sauce

1. Combine all ingredients. Mix well. Refrigerate until ready to use.

2. Serve the sauce cold with the hot fish.

Makes 6 servings

Red Cabbage and Apples

Mother always wished for cabbage on New Year's Day. Super Chef Julia Hunt's version is our favorite.

Ingredients

3 cups red cabbage, shredded (½ medium-sized cabbage)

1 ½ tablespoons balsamic vinegar

1 ½ tablespoons apple cider vinegar

1 teaspoon salt

4 slices bacon, finely chopped

½ cup onion, finely chopped (½ onion)

2 cups apples, peeled and chopped (2 large apples)

4 whole cloves

½ cup raisins

1 tablespoon brown sugar

⅛ teaspoon black pepper

1 ½ cups water

Directions

1. Mix together the cabbage, vinegar, and salt. Let stand for 30 minutes.

2. In a large saucepan with a lid, fry the bacon until brown. Add onions and cook on medium heat, stirring, for 2 or 3 minutes until the onions are soft.

3. Add cabbage, apples, cloves, raisins, sugar, pepper and water to the bacon-onion mixture in the pan. Cook on medium heat, stirring, until it comes to a boil. Then cover and cook on very low heat for 45 minutes.

4. Serve warm.

Makes 6 to 8 servings

Black-Eyed Pea Salad

Sophia Hartch provided the inspiration for this recipe. Even if you don't have Texas roots, this recipe is a winner.

Ingredients

2 cans black-eyed peas, drained (16 ounces each)

½ cup olive oil

¼ cup white vinegar, plus 1 tablespoon white vinegar

½ cup scallions, thinly sliced

2 cups tomatos, finely chopped

⅓ cup green bell pepper, finely chopped

3 tablespoons canned pickled jalapeño peppers, finely chopped

2 tablespoons fresh basil (if not available use cilantro), finely chopped

1 teaspoon coarsely ground black pepper

Directions

1. Mix all ingredients and store in the refrigerator in a covered dish overnight.

Makes 6 to 8 servings

Grandmama's Biscuits

Grandmama started the biscuits early in the day. They require less than 30 minutes of actual preparation, yet because they need to rest, this recipe takes about 4 hours. The taste and texture make these biscuits well worth the time.

Ingredients

½ cup potatoes, peeled and chopped

½ cup butter plus 2 tablespoons for brushing

¼ cup potato water, plus ½ cup potato water

1 cup milk

½ cup sugar plus 1 teaspoon to be mixed with the yeast

4½ cups flour, divided

1 teaspoon salt

1 package dry yeast (¼ ounce), not rapid-rise yeast

1 teaspoon baking powder

Note: This recipe requires a warm, draft free area to let the dough rise. An easy way to do this is to use your oven. Heat the oven to 150 degrees, turn it off, then open the door slightly to bring the inside temperature down to about 90 degrees. This makes the perfect area to let your dough rise.

Directions

1. In a small saucepan, cover potatoes with 2 cups water. Cook on medium heat until soft (approximately 12 minutes). Drain the potatoes, reserving the potato water. Thoroughly mash the potatoes in the saucepan.

2. Add butter, ¼ cup potato water, and milk to the mashed potatoes and cook on medium heat until butter melts. Mix well and remove from heat.

3. In the bowl of an electric mixer, combine the potato mixture, ½ cup sugar, 1 cup flour, and salt. Beat on medium speed for 2 to 3 minutes.

4. Dissolve yeast in ½ cup lukewarm potato water. (Be sure it has cooled. Hot water will kill the yeast.) Stir in 1 teaspoon sugar, and let stand in warm spot for 5 minutes.

5. Add the yeast mixture to the potato mixture. Beat on medium speed for about 2 minutes. Cover with a cheesecloth or thin dish towel and place in a warm, draft-free spot until bubbly (about 2 hours).

6. Sift 1 cup flour with baking powder. Add to the potato mixture. Beat on medium speed for about 2 minutes.

7. Gradually add remaining flour (2½ cups) while beating on low speed. Beat for about 3 minutes.

8. Put the dough in a greased crock to rise. Brush the top with butter. Cover and set in a warm, draft-free spot.

9. When the dough has doubled in size (about 30 minutes), knead on a lightly floured surface for 3 to 5 minutes.

10. Roll the dough out until it is about ½ inch thick. Using a cookie cutter, cut into round biscuits. Place on a greased cookie sheet, cover, and let rise in a warm, draft-free spot until about doubled in size (about 30 minutes).

Preheat oven to 350 degrees

11. Brush with melted butter and bake 15 to 20 minutes in a 350-degree oven.

Makes 24 biscuits

Lemon Mint Butter

The more mint grew on the farm, the more ways we enjoyed it. This lemony mint butter is so good you will reach for another biscuit just to have another taste.

Ingredients

1 cup soft or whipped butter

2 teaspoons lemon juice

4 tablespoons mint, finely minced

⅛ teaspoon salt (if butter is unsalted)

Directions

1. Leave butter out for 1 to 2 hours to soften.

2. Combine ingredients and mix well.

3. Put into a small crock and refrigerate for at least 1 hour before serving.

Makes 24 servings

Apple Raspberry Crisp

This recipe from my mother's Indiana kitchen is an easy, much-loved dessert.

Ingredients

6 cups apples, peeled, cored, and chopped

2 cups raspberries

1 cup sugar

4 tablespoons flour

1 ¼ teaspoons cinnamon

Ingredients for the Topping

¾ cup quick-cooking oats

⅓ cup flour

⅓ cup brown sugar, packed

½ cup butter, melted

Directions

Preheat the oven to 350 degrees.

1. Mix the apples, raspberries, sugar, flour, and cinnamon.

2. Put the apple mixture into a lightly greased 9 x 12 inch baking dish.

3. Combine the topping ingredients and mix well. Spread this mixture on top of the apples.

4. Bake for 35 minutes.

Makes 8 to 10 servings

Restoring Health

Prayer at a Meal to Restore Health

Dear God,

We come to you now as children in need. You are the Great Physician who can heal and provide health to all those whom you choose. You know our needs better than we know them ourselves, and you know what we need more than anything is a healthy relationship with you. You can provide physical healing, but more importantly, you can provide spiritual healing. We pray now that you would use this food that we are about to eat to bring strength to our bodies and nourishment to our souls. This we ask in the power of the Spirit and your Son, Jesus Christ. Amen.

Prayer by Tom Harris

Bible Verses

Restore us, O Lord God Almighty; make your face shine upon us, that we may be saved. (Psalm 80:19)

. . . I will restore you to health and heal your wounds. (Jeremiah 30:17)

Dear friend, I pray that you may enjoy good health and that all may go well with you, even as your soul is getting along well. (3 John 1:2)

Menu

```
Grandmother's Chicken Soup
Potato Sidekicks
Raspberry Orange Salad
Float
Ginger Tea
```

Grandmother's Chicken Soup

Even the smell of this soup seems filled with healing power. Enjoy a bowlful and you are bound to feel restored and on the way to a healthy recovery.

Ingredients

2 cups raw or cooked chicken, chopped into small pieces

5 cups chicken broth

1 cup celery, finely chopped

1 cup carrots, peeled and chopped into thin rounds

1 ½ tablespoons garlic, peeled and finely minced

½ cup onion, peeled and finely chopped

¼ teaspoon ground sage

¼ teaspoon ground thyme

½ cup rice

salt and freshly ground pepper to taste

Directions

1. In a large cooking pot, combine all of the ingredients.

2. Bring to a boil, stir, and then lower the heat.

3. Cover the pot and cook on low heat for 30 minutes, stirring occasionally.

Makes 6 to 8 servings

Potato Sidekicks

Baked in a muffin pan, these are just right to enjoy with chicken soup or any other meal for that matter. Filled with potatoes, they are astonishingly light.

Ingredients

3 cups grated raw potatoes

3 eggs

½ cup sifted flour

½ teaspoon baking powder

½ teaspoon salt

¼ cup melted butter

Directions

Preheat oven to 400 degrees.

1. Grate potatoes, pat dry, and place in a large mixing bowl.
2. Separate eggs, reserving the whites.
3. Beat egg yolks and mix into the grated potatoes.
4. Sift together flour, baking powder, and salt. Add to potatoes and mix well.
5. Beat egg whites until stiff and fold into the potato mixture.
6. Fill muffin pan cups two-thirds full.
7. Bake at 400 degrees for 25 minutes.
8. Serve immediately.

Makes 14 to 18 sidekicks

Raspberry Orange Salad

The cranberry juice blends magically with the flavored gelatins creating this refreshing salad.

Ingredients

1 package orange gelatin, 3 ounces

1 package raspberry gelatin, 3 ounces

⅛ teaspoon cinnamon

2 cups boiling water

2 cups cranberry juice

1 cup oranges, peeled, seeded, and finely chopped

1 cup raspberries

Directions

1. Dissolve the orange and raspberry gelatin and cinnamon in boiling water. Stir 1 or 2 minutes until the gelatin is completely dissolved.

2. Add the cranberry juice and chill until slightly thickened (about 1 ½ hours).

3. Add the oranges and raspberries to the slightly thickened gelatin and continue to cool until firm (about another 2 ½ hours).

Makes 6 to 8 servings

Float

In my earliest kitchen memories, I am standing on a step stool, stirring the Float (sometimes called "Floating Islands"). I have always loved this job and this soothing dessert.

Ingredients

4 eggs

2 tablespoons flour

¾ cup sugar

4 cups milk

1 teaspoon vanilla extract

Directions

1. Separate eggs, placing the yolks in the top of a double boiler and the whites in the bowl of an electric mixer.

2. Beat yolks with a wire whisk or rotary beater. Add the flour and sugar and mix well. Stir the milk into the mixture.

3. Cook the yolk-milk mixture in the double boiler. Do not boil. Stir the mixture frequently and remove from heat when it thickens (approximately 30 minutes).

4. Toward the end of the cooking of the yolk mixture, beat egg whites in the electric mixer until stiff. Add vanilla. Continue beating until well mixed.

5. Pour the hot mixture into the egg whites. Stir while pouring.

6. This is delicious warm and can be served right away. It's also good refrigerated and served cold.

Makes 6 to 8 servings

Ginger Tea

When Grandmother replaced castor oil with ginger tea, the whole family felt better. Centuries of use in Asia confirm its health benefits. I drink it just because I like it.

Ingredients

Green tea (1 teaspoon loose or 1 tea bag)

3 slices fresh ginger or candied ginger

Directions

1. Pour hot water (375 degrees) over the tea and the ginger.

2. Steep for 4 to 6 minutes.

For more detailed tea making directions, see Page 208.

Makes 1 cup

<u>Notes</u>

Retirement Party

Prayer at a Retirement Party

Dear Heavenly Father,

Everything has a beginning and an end. As _____ comes to the end of this chapter of his/her life, we ask that this new beginning bring even more excitement and anticipation of the future than he/she could ever have imagined! May he/she be off and running, not turning back. God has wonderful plans for each moment of our lives to give us a hope and a future. May we remember the life lessons from the road already traveled and may they be stepping stones and not stumbling blocks in the days ahead. Thank you for newness in life. Keep _____ on the right track with a clear vision of the goals he/she has. There is far more to life out there. With renewed strength and loving guidance from you, life is good! We love and praise you. In your almighty name. Amen.

Prayer by Marty Harris Butler

Bible Verses

In your unfailing love you will lead the people you have redeemed. In your strength you will guide them to your holy dwelling. (Exodus 15:13)

You have made known to me the path of life; you will fill me with joy in your presence, with eternal pleasures at your right hand. (Psalm 16:11)

Menu

Aunt Pearl's Chicken and Dumplings
Green Beans with Herbs
Carrot Casserole
Cranberry Peanut Coleslaw
Blueberry Banana Cream Pie

Aunt Pearl's Chicken and Dumplings

Aunt Pearl's dumplings are a treasured inheritance. Pearl was born in 1882 in Indiana. Two generations later, imagine my delight when I made these dumplings for my Texas-born husband, who said, "This is exactly the way dumplings should be." Aunt Pearl canned her own chicken broth. If you have time, you may want to do this, too.

Ingredients

1 chicken or your favorite chicken parts

5½ cups chicken broth, canned

Ingredients for the Dumplings

2 cups sifted flour

½ cup lard or vegetable shortening

1 level teaspoon baking powder

½ teaspoon salt

1 egg, beaten

¼ cup milk

2 tablespoons flour

Directions

1. In a large cooking pot, cover the chicken with water and cook on medium-low heat until tender. Remove chicken from the pot. When it is cool enough to handle, remove the bones and cut the chicken into small pieces. Save the chicken broth.

2. In a bowl, combine flour, lard or shortening, baking powder, and salt. Using a fork or fingers, mix together until the mixture is like corn meal.

3. Stirring with a fork, add beaten egg and slowly pour milk into the mixture. Add just enough milk to hold the mixture together (¼ cup milk is usually just right).

4. With your fingers, form the dough into a ball. The dough should be kind of tough.

5. On floured waxed paper, roll the ball until thin. Sprinkle 2 tablespoons flour over the dough, and using your hands, spread the flour evenly over the dough.

6. Cut dough into 1½ inch squares.

7. Bring chicken broth to a boil (combine fresh broth with the canned broth).

8. One at a time, drop the squares into the boiling broth. They will drop to the bottom and then float to the top.

9. As soon as all the squares are in the pot, cook on medium heat for 5 to 6 minutes, stirring occasionally. Then return the chicken to the pot.

10. Remove from heat when the chicken is hot.

Makes 8 servings

Green Beans with Herbs

Be sure not to overcook the beans. They should be crispy. Whenever possible, use fresh herbs.

Ingredients

4 cups fresh green beans

½ cup scallions, finely chopped

1 ½ tablespoons olive oil

1 teaspoon dry oregano (1 tablespoon fresh)

1 teaspoon dry basil (2 tablespoons fresh)

¼ teaspoon dry marjoram

½ cup fresh parsley, finely chopped

Directions

1. Rinse and drain the beans. Cut off the ends and cut in half.

2. In a pan with a tight lid, combine the beans with two cups water. Cover and cook on medium-high heat for 10 minutes. Remove from heat and drain.

3. In a small skillet, combine olive oil and scallions. Cook on medium heat for 2 to 3 minutes until the scallions are soft.

4. Add any dry herbs (oregano, basil, marjoram) to the scallions and continue to cook, stirring for 2 to 3 minutes.

5. Combine the drained beans, cooked scallion mixture, parsley, and any fresh herbs. Mix well. Serve hot.

Makes 6 to 8 servings

Carrot Casserole

This unusual side dish was created for a family competition. It is a tasty variation of old-fashioned carrot salad.

Ingredients

⅓ cup dark brown sugar

3 tablespoons butter

4 eggs

½ cup flour

½ teaspoon baking powder

¼ teaspoon salt

¼ teaspoon curry powder

¾ cup light cream

½ cup raisins

2 cups carrots, grated

Directions

Pre-heat the oven to 350 degrees.

1. In the bowl of an electric mixer, combine the sugar and butter. Mix well.

2. Separate the egg yolks from the egg whites. Reserve the whites. Add the egg yolks to the mixture. Mix well.

3. Sift together the flour, baking powder, salt, and curry powder.

4. Beating on low speed, add the flour mixture and light cream. Mix well and then stir in the raisins and carrots.

5. In a separate bowl, beat egg whites until stiff peaks form.

6. Gently stir the beaten egg whites into the carrot mixture.

7. Pour mixture into a greased 8 x 8 inch baking dish. Bake for 35 minutes.

Makes 6 to 8 servings

Cranberry Peanut Coleslaw

For my mother, this was the coleslaw that topped them all. The secret ingredient is the coconut.

Ingredients for the Coleslaw

4 cups green cabbage, grated (about ½ cabbage)

¾ cup salted peanuts, roughly chopped

¾ cup dried cranberries

2 tablespoons shredded coconut

Ingredients for the Dressing

½ cup mayonnaise

3 tablespoons apple cider vinegar

1 tablespoon sugar

1 tablespoon light cream

½ teaspoon salt

Directions

1. Combine grated cabbage, peanuts, cranberries, and coconut.

2. To prepare the dressing, combine the mayonnaise, vinegar, sugar, cream, and salt. Mix well.

3. Stir the dressing into the cabbage mixture. Mix well.

Makes 6 to 8 servings

Blueberry Banana Cream Pie

Cousin Susan is renowned for her delicious pies. Her welcome arrival, usually with several pies, always delights us. This unusual combination of blueberries and bananas is her husband's favorite!

Ingredients for the Crust

1 cup flour, un-sifted

⅓ cup shortening

⅛ teaspoon salt

¼ cup ice water

Directions for the Crust

Preheat the oven to 350 degrees.

1. In a bowl, combine flour, shortening and salt. Using a fork or fingers mix together until the mixture is like corn meal.

2. Stirring with a fork, slowly pour ice water into the flour. With your fingers form the dough into a ball. If the dough is too dry to form a ball, add a tiny bit more water. Let the dough rest for 15 minutes.

3. On floured waxed paper, roll the ball into a circle. Fold the dough and paper gently in half and slip the dough off the paper and into a pie plate.

4. Trim the overlapping edge with a knife and then crimp the edge with your fingers. Using a fork, prick lots of tiny holes in the bottom of the crust.

5. Bake in a 350-degree oven for 15 minutes. Remove from oven and cool.

Blueberry Banana Cream Pie

Ingredients for the Filling

3 bananas, sliced into thin rounds

1 teaspoon lemon juice

1 cup blueberries, washed, drained, and patted dry with paper towels

¾ cup sugar

⅓ cup flour

⅛ teaspoon salt

2 cups milk

3 egg yolks, beaten

1 ½ tablespoons butter, cut into pieces

1 teaspoon vanilla extract

Directions for the Filling

1. Mix sliced bananas with lemon juice and spread on the bottom of the baked cooled pie crust. Cover with the blueberries.

2. In a heavy saucepan, combine the sugar, flour, and salt. Mix well. Slowly stir the milk into the mixture.

3. On medium heat, while stirring, bring the mixture to a boil. Continue to stir and let boil for 1 minute. Remove from heat.

4. Slowly pour ½ cup of the hot mixture into the beaten egg yolks. Mix well and then stir the egg yolks into the hot mixture in the saucepan. Stirring vigorously, return the mixture to a boil. Remove from heat.

5. Stir the butter and vanilla into the hot mixture. Mix well. Pour immediately into the pie crust on top of the bananas and blueberries.

6. Cover the filling with wax paper and cool in the refrigerator for at least 1 hour before covering with whipped cream.

Blueberry Banana Cream Pie

Ingredients for the Topping

1 cup cold heavy cream

1 tablespoon confectioners sugar

Directions for the Topping

1. Using a rotary beater, beat together the cream and sugar until soft peaks form.

2. Spread whipped cream on top of cooled pie.

Makes 1 pie

Tea Party

Prayer at a Tea Party

Precious God,

Thank you for this delightful gathering of friends. The gift of friendship here on earth is a taste of the life that one day we will be living in your heavenly kingdom. While we are here, we ask that our conversation be filled with love, grace, and fellowship. May we strive to live lives that honor and glorify you. We are thankful for the food before us, the times we share, and the simple joys we so readily take for granted: health, home, and plenty. Give us gracious hearts. In Christ's beloved name, and for his gift of eternal life, we say thank you and seek your blessing on our conversation and our lives. Amen.

Prayer by Barbara Harris Youngflesh

Bible Verse

. . . whatever is true, whatever is noble, whatever is just, whatever is right, whatever is pure, whatever is lovely, whatever is admirable—if anything is excellent or praiseworthy— think about such things .
(Philippians 4:8)

Menu

Sandwiches
 Apricot Banana Sandwiches
 Cucumber Sandwiches
 Date Nut Cream Cheese Sandwiches
 Ham Salad Sandwiches
Lemon Tea Party Cake
Mexican Wedding Cakes
Chocolate Covered Strawberries
Proper Tea

Tea Sandwiches

Tea sandwiches are little sandwiches with varied fillings. Very thin bread is a must and the crust should be cut off. Each type of sandwich should be cut into a different shape- squares, triangles, circles, rectangles.

Ingredients for Apricot Banana Sandwiches

4 slices raisin bread, with crust removed

¼ cup apricot preserves

½ small banana, peeled and cut into thin rounds

¼ teaspoon lemon juice

1 tablespoon soft butter

Directions for Apricot Banana Sandwiches

1. Spread two slices of bread with apricot preserves (See Orange, Apricot, Peach Conserve on page 148).

2. Sprinkle the bananas with the lemon juice and then place the bananas on top of the preserves.

3. Spread butter on the remaining slices and cover.

4. Cut each sandwich into 4 pieces (a square).

Makes 8 small sandwiches

Ingredients for Cucumber Sandwiches

8 slices thin white bread with crust removed

¼ cup mayonnaise

1 teaspoon soft butter

½ small cucumber, peeled, thinly sliced

2 tablespoons parsley, finely minced

⅛ scant teaspoon salt

Directions for Cucumber Sandwiches

1. Spread 4 slices of bread with mayonnaise and 4 slices of bread with butter.

2. Place the cucumber slices on the buttered bread and sprinkle with parsley and salt. Cover with the mayonnaise bread.

3. Cut each sandwich into 4 triangular pieces.

Makes 16 small sandwiches

Tea Sandwiches

Ingredients for Date Nut Cream Cheese Sandwiches

6 thin slices date nut bread (often available in small, round loaves)

¾ cup soft cream cheese

Directions for Date Nut Cream Cheese Sandwiches

1. Spread date nut bread slices with cream cheese.

2. Cover and cut into small pie shaped pieces.

Makes 12 small sandwiches

Ingredients for Ham Salad Sandwiches

6 slices thin whole wheat bread, with crust removed

½ cup cooked ham, chopped

1 hardboiled egg

3 small sweet pickles

1 ½ tablespoons mayonnaise (add more if needed)

Directions for Ham Salad Sandwiches

1. In a food processor, combine ham, egg, pickles, and mayonnaise. Mix well.

2. Spread on 3 slices of bread. Cover with the remaining slices.

3. Cut each sandwich into six rectangular pieces.

Makes 18 small sandwiches

Lemon Tea Party Cake

When you read this recipe you probably won't believe it will be any good. Passed down for three generations, it's not just good – it's great! We couldn't help leaving Grandmother's sour cream instructions.

Ingredients for the Cake

1 cup sugar

1½ cups flour

1 egg, break into a measuring cup. Finish filling with sour cream to the 1 cup level.

1 teaspoon lemon extract

½ teaspoon soda

Directions for the Cake

Preheat oven to 350 degrees.

1. Put all ingredients together and mix well.

2. Bake in a greased and floured 8 x 8 inch baking pan. Bake for 25 to 30 minutes.

Ingredients for the Icing

2 cups confectioners sugar

¼ cup butter

4 tablespoons frozen concentrate orange juice

Directions for the Icing

1. Beat sugar and butter together until creamy. Add orange juice, mixing well. Spread on the cooled cake.

Makes 12 tea party servings

Mexican Wedding Cakes

Really a cookie, these delicate sweets share all our special occasions.

Ingredients

1 cup soft butter

½ cup confectioners sugar

¼ teaspoon salt

2 teaspoons vanilla extract

2 cups sifted flour

1 ½ cup pecans, very finely chopped

¾ cup confectioners sugar, for dusting after baking

Directions

Preheat oven to 350 degrees.

1. In the bowl of an electric mixer, combine butter and ½ cup confectioners sugar. Beat until creamy.

2. Add salt, vanilla, flour, and nuts. Mix well. Refrigerate the dough for at least 1 hour.

3. Using your fingers, shape the dough into 1-inch balls. Place the balls on an un-greased cookie sheet.

4. Bake in a 350-degree oven for 12 to 15 minutes until lightly brown.

5. Spread the confectioners sugar in a pie plate. While the cookies are hot, gently remove from the baking sheet and place in the confectioners sugar. Using your fingers, sprinkle sugar on top and sides.

Makes 45 to 50 small cookies

Chocolate Covered Strawberries

Our family loves chocolate covered strawberries. In my recipe, the chocolate on the berry stays firm without becoming brittle.

Ingredients

24 strawberries

Directions for Preparing the Strawberries

1. Wash the strawberries and cut off the stem ends.

2. Let dry at room temperature.

Ingredients for the Chocolate Dipping Mixture

1 cup premium semi-sweet chocolate chips

1 tablespoon premium unsweetened cocoa

3 tablespoons heavy cream

Directions

1. In the top of a double boiler, heat the chocolate chips, cocoa, and cream until melted. Stir frequently until well mixed. Remove from heat.

2. Spear the strawberry on the stem end. Dip the strawberry in the hot chocolate mixture. When coated, place the strawberry on a serving plate stem end down.

3. When all of the strawberries are coated, refrigerate for about 20 to 30 minutes to let the chocolate cool. Don't leave in the refrigerator more than a few hours or the chocolate will begin to sweat.

4. Serve cool within a day.

Makes 24 strawberries

Proper Tea

Offer a cup of tea, some little sandwiches and sweets, and everyone will relax and have a good time. Choose your favorite tea. My two favorites are jasmine green tea and Earl Grey.

Directions for Jasmine Green Tea

1. Fill the kettle with cold water. Place on medium heat. Bring to a boil and then remove from heat and let it rest 1 to 2 minutes, to reach the right temperature of 180 to 190 degrees. (Have your teapot ready so the hot water can be poured on the tea immediately.)

2. Rinse your teapot with hot water. Place in the pot one teaspoon of loose tea (or one tea bag) for every 6 ounces of water. Ideally, loose tea would be placed in a large tea ball infuser. Pour the hot water over the tea. Place the lid on the teapot and let the tea brew for several minutes. I leave my jasmine green tea in the pot for 4 minutes. The better the tea, the longer you can leave it without it becoming bitter. Tea bags cannot be left in as long as loose tea and do not produce as good a flavor.

3. Remove the tea ball or tea bags or strain the loose tea and return strained tea to the pot.

4. Just before serving, open the pot, stir and then pour. If the tea is too strong, add hot water.

Directions for Earl Grey Tea

Follow the instructions for Jasmine Green Tea, with the following changes:

1. Use 1 heaping teaspoon of loose tea for every 6 ounces of water and one for the pot.

2. Pour the freshly boiled water directly over the tea.

3. Steep for 6 minutes.

4. If you take milk with your tea, add it to the cup cold before pouring the tea.

<u>Notes</u>

Thanksgiving

Prayer at Thanksgiving

Almighty God,

All things good come at your bidding. Your mercy and grace know no bounds. On this day of Thanksgiving, we could never thank you enough for what you have done for each of us. Every blessing that we enjoy is a gift from you. There is nothing that we have that your hand has not provided. You have allowed us to live in a country where we possess liberty and freedoms that many do not share. Let us never forget the source of our blessings, Jesus Christ, and for that we should be eternally grateful. We ask that this food be blessed and that we always be thankful to the One who is the Great Provider. In Christ we pray. Amen.

Prayer by Tom Harris

Bible Verse

I will praise you, O Lord with all my whole heart; I will tell of all your wonders. (Psalm 9:1)

Menu

Turkey with Giblet Gravy
Chestnut Stuffing
Corn Pudding
Mashed Potatoes
Scalloped Oysters
Cranberry Coconut Bread
Cranberry Orange Salad
Pumpkin Pie
Sweet Potato Pie

Turkey with Giblet Gravy

Maybe because Grandmother always prepared our chicken and turkey dinners by first killing the bird and then dressing and cleaning it, taking special care to draw out the pin feathers, our appreciation and preparation of the bird has always been a simple one. (The Giblet Gravy is the next recipe.)

Ingredients

Choose a fresh turkey, not a frozen one.

Directions for Roasting the Turkey

Preheat oven to 325 degrees

1. Wash the turkey inside and out, pat it dry, and then rub the outside with butter.

2. Sprinkle with salt and pepper, place in a roasting pan breast up, and cover it loosely with foil.

3. Roast in a 325-degree oven for 2 to 4 hours depending on the size of the bird. Standard cooking time for turkeys is 15 minutes per pound.

4. About every 30 minutes while baking, baste the turkey with the juices in the pan and with melted butter.

5. In the last 15 to 20 minutes, remove the foil so the turkey will brown.

Makes 1 serving per pound of turkey

Giblet Gravy

Giblets are the heart, kidney, gizzard, and the liver of the turkey. Often these parts are in a bag and tucked inside the bird. Gravy made with these edible parts is rich and delicious.

Ingredients

Giblets (include the neck but not the liver)

3 cups water

½ cup juice from the roasting turkey

2 tablespoons butter

3 ½ tablespoons flour

1 ¾ cups milk, heated (hot to the touch but not boiling)

Directions

1. In a saucepan combine the giblets and water. Cover and cook on low heat for 1 hour.

2. Remove meat from the neck and cut neck meat and giblets into very small pieces.

3. In a saucepan combine ½ cup turkey juice from the roasting pan, butter, and flour. Stirring vigorously, cook on medium heat for 3 to 4 minutes.

4. While stirring, add one cup of the giblet broth and the heated milk. Continue to cook on medium heat, stirring until the mixture begins to thicken.

5. Remove from heat, add giblet pieces, and serve hot.

Makes 8 servings

Chestnut Stuffing

Rather than stuff the turkey, we like this dish all on its own. My daughter,
Gwendolyn, was the inspiration for this recipe.

Ingredients

1½ cups canned, dry whole chestnuts (about 7 ounces).

5 cups cubed white bread (French or homemade style)

2 cups butternut squash, peeled and chopped into very small cubes.

1 cup chopped celery

2 cups chopped onions

2 tablespoons finely chopped fresh sage leaves

1 tablespoon finely chopped fresh thyme leaves

2 tablespoons finely chopped fresh rosemary

1 teaspoon dried savory

½ cup butter

1 cup chicken or vegetable broth, divided

1 teaspoon salt

½ teaspoon ground pepper

Directions

Preheat oven to 350 degrees.

1. Chop each chestnut into 4 pieces.
2. Arrange bread in one layer in a baking dish and bake, stirring occasionally until lightly browned (about 20 minutes).
3. In a frying pan, combine the squash, celery, onion, sage, thyme, rosemary, savory, and butter. Fry on low heat, stirring frequently, until the onions are soft.
4. Combine the chestnuts, bread, onion mixture, salt, pepper, and ½ cup broth. Mix well and place in a 13 x 8 inch baking dish. Bake for approximately 40 minutes. About every 10 minutes stir and add additional broth.

Makes 8 to 10 servings

Corn Pudding

When sweet corn is in season, put some up in the freezer. You will want this easy to make comfort food- on Thanksgiving and probably Christmas, too!

Ingredients

1 tablespoon flour

1 tablespoon sugar

1 tablespoon butter, room temperature

3 eggs

1 teaspoon salt

1 cup milk

½ cup heavy cream

2 cups fresh corn (cut off the cob) or frozen corn

Directions

Preheat oven to 325 degrees.

1. In the bowl of an electric mixer, combine flour, sugar, butter, eggs, and salt. Beat on medium speed until blended.

2. Stir the milk, heavy cream, and corn into the mixture.

3. Pour the corn mixture into a buttered 6-cup, deep baking dish. Place the dish in a shallow pan of water.

4. Bake in a 325-degree oven for 1 ½ hours or until a knife inserted in the center comes out clean.

Makes 6 servings

Mashed Potatoes

My father, Maurice Hunt, always mashed the potatoes. No one else could do it just right. What kind of potatoes do you use? "You know those ordinary ones." So we followed him to the store and he picked up a bag of Yukon Gold potatoes. His secrets - mash while potatoes are hot, heat the milk with the butter, and whip it into the potatoes - and "of course, use a ricer, how else could you do it?"

Ingredients

10 potatoes, medium size

1 cup heavy cream

1 ¼ cups milk

1 teaspoon salt

¼ cup butter

Directions

1. Peel potatoes, cut into quarters, and place in large pan. Cover with water.

2. Bring to a boil and then lower heat and simmer until potatoes are tender (about 15 minutes).

3. In a small saucepan, combine milk, salt and butter. Heat until the butter melts.

4. Place the hot potatoes in the ricer and quickly mash all of the potatoes.

5. Pour the hot milk mixture into the hot potatoes, whipping the potatoes as you pour.

6. Add a little more cream if the potatoes are stiff. Taste for salt. You may wish for more.

Makes 8 to 10 servings

Scalloped Oysters

Oysters have been a special treat for generations past, enjoyed by American Indians and early colonists. This dish is greatly looked forward to on our Thanksgiving table.

Ingredients

1½ pints oysters

2 cups cracker crumbs

½ cup butter

1 ½ cups milk

Directions

Preheat oven to 350 degrees.

1. Drain and check the oysters for any shell pieces, which must be discarded.

2. Into a deep buttered casserole dish, place a layer of cracker crumbs, cover with oysters and little slivers of butter.

3. Repeat layers, ending with a layer of cracker crumbs topped with small slivers of butter.

4. Punch holes in the layered mixture. Pour the milk on top of the casserole to fill the holes.

5. Bake at 350 degrees for approximately 40 minutes, until top is slightly brown.

Makes 6 to 8 servings

Cranberry Coconut Bread

We love cranberries and coconut.

Ingredients

¼ cup butter

1 cup sugar

1 egg

2 cups flour

½ teaspoon baking soda

1 ½ teaspoons baking powder

¼ teaspoon salt

¾ cup orange juice

1½ cups cranberries, roughly chopped

¾ cup flaked coconut

½ cup pecans, chopped

Directions

Preheat oven to 350 degrees.

1. In the bowl of an electric mixer, combine the butter and sugar. Beat until creamy. Add egg. Mix well.

2. Sift together flour, baking soda, baking powder, and salt in a separate bowl.

3. Alternating juice and flour, combine with the sugar mixture. Mix well.

4. Stir in the cranberries, coconut, and nuts.

5. Spoon into a greased 9 x 5 inch loaf pan. Bake at 350 degrees for 50 to 60 minutes. Insert toothpick in center. When it comes out clean, the bread is done.

6. Drizzle Orange Glaze over the hot bread (see next recipe).

Makes 1 loaf (14 slices)

Orange Glaze

Ingredients

½ cup confectioners sugar

2 tablespoons frozen orange juice concentrate

Directions

1. Combine sugar and orange juice. Mix until smooth.

2. Drizzle over hot bread.

Cranberry Orange Salad

With a food processor, this is a quick cranberry dish using raw cranberries and oranges. It is refreshing and delicious! We keep packages of frozen cranberries so we can serve this salad throughout the year.

Ingredients

4 cups cranberries

3 cups oranges, peeled, seeded, and finely chopped

¾ cup sugar

½ cup pecans, roughly chopped

Directions

1. Using a food processor, process cranberries for a few seconds until they are roughly chopped. Place in a bowl.

2. Process the oranges for a few seconds.

3. Combine all the ingredients. Mix well.

Makes 8 to 10 servings

Pie Crusts for Pumpkin and Sweet Potato Pies

Pie crusts are so personal. State Fair judges and magazine contests will never sort out the one and only very best. Our blue ribbon goes to mother's thin, light, flaky crust.

Ingredients

3 cups flour un-sifted

1 cup shortening

⅛ teaspoon salt

½ cup plus 2 tablespoons ice water

Directions

1. In a bowl, combine flour, shortening and salt. Using a fork or fingers, mix together until the texture is like corn meal.

2. Stirring with a fork, slowly pour ice water into the flour. With your fingers form the dough into 3 balls. (If too dry to form balls, add a tiny bit more water). Let dough rest for 15 minutes.

3. On floured wax paper, roll out each ball into a circle. Fold paper and dough in half and slip dough off the paper into a pie plate.

4. Trim the overlapping edges with a knife and then crimp edges with your fingers. Using a fork, prick lots of tiny holes in the crust.

Makes 3 pie crusts

Pumpkin Pie

Made with fresh Sugar Pumpkin - from the garden is best! Do not use Jack-O-Lantern ones. Pumpkin pieces can be placed in a shallow bowl of water in the microwave and cooked. Then remove the shell and puree in a blender. If you are using very juicy freshly cooked pumpkin, add only ¼ cup milk to the mixture.

Ingredients

1½ cups cooked sugar pumpkin

½ cup light brown sugar

¼ cup sugar

½ cup milk

¼ cup heavy cream

2 eggs, beaten

½ teaspoon cinnamon

½ teaspoon nutmeg

⅛ teaspoon salt

Directions

Preheat oven to 425 degrees.

1. Combine all of the ingredients. Mix well.

2. Pour mixture into an un-baked pie crust (page 202).

3. Bake at 425 degrees for the first 15 minutes.

4. Lower the oven heat to 400 degrees and continue to bake for approximately 20 more minutes. Pie is ready when the center of the pumpkin custard is slightly firm.

Makes 1 pie

Sweet Potato Pie

Grandmama Ora Hunt wrote, "I have no written recipe for sweet potato pie. I will try to tell you how. I hope you can learn to make them, as they are good, especially when the sweet potatoes are just dug from the garden."

Ingredients

3 sweet potatoes, medium sized

2 tablespoons flour

1 cup sugar, divided

⅛ teaspoon salt

¼ cup butter, cut into little pieces

1 teaspoon allspice, divided

½ to ⅔ cup water

2 un-baked pie crusts (one for the cover), see page 220

Directions

Preheat oven to 350 degrees.

1. Boil the sweet potatoes with the skins on until tender. Remove the skins and slice the potatoes into thin slices (approximately ¼ inch thick).

2. Combine the flour, salt, and ½ cup of the sugar. Sprinkle the flour-sugar mixture into the un-baked pie crust, covering the bottom.

3. Place a layer of sliced potatoes into the pie. Dot the layer with pieces of butter. Sprinkle with some allspice.

4. Add a second layer of potatoes. Dot with butter and sprinkle with allspice. Pour the remaining sugar over the pie.

5. Gently pour water into the pie. (Grandmama said "pour in as much water as you can to keep the pie moist, but the trick is, not to pour in so much that the pie cooks over".)

6. Cover the pie with a top crust. Pinch edges together and make a few cuts in the top for air to vent.

7. Bake at 350 degrees for approximately 45 to 60 minutes. Pie should be lightly browned.

Makes 1 pie

<u>Notes</u>

Valentine's Day

Prayer on Valentine's Day

Dear Heavenly Father,

Wow! There are no words to truly describe love. Love is confusing. It makes us sooooo happy but at times, it can cause us pain. Today we rejoice in love. Help us to live in the moment - to be thankful for each person who has loved us and for those we have loved. If we love one another, God dwells deeply within us and his love becomes complete in us---perfect love! Help us to reflect your sweet love in everything we say and do and forgive us for the times our words and deeds have made you sad. What a special day to reflect and remember that God is Love! In your loving name. Amen.

Prayer by Marty Harris Butler

Bible Verse

Dear friends, let us love one another, for love comes from God. Everyone who loves had been born of God and knows God. Whoever does not love does not know God, because God is love. This is how God showed his love among us: He sent his one and only Son into the world that we might live through him. This is love: not that we loved God, but that he loved us and sent his Son as an atoning sacrifice for our sins. Dear friends, since God so loved us, we also ought to love one another. No one has ever seen God; but if we love one another, God lives in us, and his love is made complete in us. (1 John 4:7-12)

Menu

> Chicken Curry
> Coconut Rice
> Honey Lime Fruit Salad
> Chocolate Mousse
> Panna Cotta
> Sweet Lassi

Chicken Curry

Make this curry the day before or early in the morning of the party. The chicken, apples, raisins, and cranberries need time to bathe in this flavorful mixture.

Ingredients

1 ½ pounds chicken

2 tablespoons curry powder

2 tablespoons flour

½ teaspoon salt

⅓ cup vegetable oil

1 cup onions, peeled and very thinly sliced (1 medium sized onion)

1 ½ teaspoons garlic, finely minced

2 cups apples, cored, peeled, and chopped (about 2 apples)

½ cup dried currants or raisins

½ cup dried cranberries

1 tablespoon dark brown sugar

1 tablespoon Worcestershire sauce

½ lemon, very thinly sliced and cut into fourths (seeds removed)

¾ cup canned coconut milk (stir well before measuring)

2 cups chicken broth

Chicken Curry

Directions

1. Remove the chicken skin and cut chicken into bite-sized pieces.

2. Mix together curry powder, flour, and salt. Add chicken pieces, stirring to coat each piece with the curry mixture.

3. In a large heavy saucepan, heat the oil reserving 3 tablespoons (for cooking the onions and garlic later). Add chicken pieces and curry mixture to hot oil. Cook, stirring on medium-low heat for 3 minutes.

4. In a frying pan, combine the remaining 3 tablespoons oil, onions and garlic. Cook, stirring, on medium heat until onions begin to turn translucent.

5. Add apples to onions and continue to cook, stirring for 3 minutes.

6. Combine the onion and apple mixture with the chicken in the heavy saucepan and add the remaining ingredients.

7. Bring to a boil, then lower heat, cover, and simmer for 1 hour.

Makes 8 to 10 servings

Coconut Rice

A favorite of ours: you may discover this is your signature rice. The addition of coconut gives a subtle, oh-so-delicious flavor, cheering many menus.

Ingredients

3 cups rice

1 cup canned coconut milk

5 cups water

¼ teaspoon salt

¾ cup shredded coconut (reserve ¼ cup for garnish)

Directions

1. In a saucepan combine the rice, coconut milk, water, salt, and shredded coconut. On medium high heat, bring to a boil.

2. Stir with a fork, lower heat, and cover with a tight fitting lid. Continue to cook on low heat for 14 minutes.

3. Garnish with shredded coconut. Serve hot.

Makes 8 to 10 servings

Honey Lime Fruit Salad

The dressing on this refreshing fruit salad is a gift from my culinary friend Janice Donnelly.

Ingredients for the Salad

2 cups oranges, peeled, seeded, and finely chopped

1 cup grapes, sliced in half

2 cups pineapple, finely chopped

1 cup strawberries, sliced

2 cups mixed lettuce greens (choose a mixture with a red leaf lettuce)

1 cup walnuts, roughly chopped

Ingredients for the Dressing

1 cup plain yogurt

1 tablespoon lime juice

1 tablespoon lime zest, finely chopped

3 tablespoons honey

Directions

1. Mix together the oranges, grapes, pineapple, and strawberries.

2. Prepare the dressing by combining all the ingredients. Mix well.

3. Arrange lettuce on each salad plate. Place a mound of fruit mixture on top of the greens. Swirl dressing generously on each salad. Garnish with walnuts.

Makes 8 to 10 servings

Chocolate Mousse with Raspberry Sauce

This fluffy mousse with raspberry sauce is one of my husband's favorites.

Ingredients for the Mousse

12 ounces semi-sweet chocolate

6 egg whites (large eggs)

½ teaspoon cream of tartar

⅛ teaspoon salt

3 cups heavy cream

1 teaspoon vanilla

Ingredients for Raspberry Sauce

2 cups raspberries (reserve some whole raspberries for garnish)

4 tablespoons superfine sugar

Directions for Mousse

1. In the top of a double boiler, melt the chocolate. Remove from heat and cool to lukewarm.
2. In the bowl of an electric mixer, combine the egg whites, cream of tartar, and salt. Beat on medium speed until the egg whites hold stiff peaks.
3. In a separate bowl, combine the heavy cream and vanilla. Beat until the cream holds stiff peaks.
4. Fold the chocolate gently into the egg whites. Then fold in the cream.
5. Spoon the chocolate mixture into small bowls (ramekins). Cool.

Directions for Raspberry Sauce

1. Puree the raspberries and strain through a fine sieve. Then stir in the sugar until dissolved.
2. Pour the raspberry sauce over each mousse and garnish with whole raspberries.

Makes 8 to 10 servings

Panna Cotta with Raspberry Sauce

On Valentine's Day, we often indulge in two desserts - one chocolate, one vanilla. This recipe was a gift to us by Raphael Dequeker, a talented pastry chef.

Ingredients for the Panna Cotta

4 cups heavy cream

⅔ cup sugar

1 vanilla bean

3 teaspoons gelatin (approximately 1 ¼ envelopes)

½ cup cold milk

Directions for Panna Cotta

1. In a heavy saucepan, combine cream, the sugar, and vanilla bean seeds (split the vanilla bean lengthwise, scrape out the seeds, and whisk into the cream mixture). Warm on medium heat, stirring occasionally. Be careful not to boil the mixture.

2. Sprinkle the gelatin over the cold milk in a bowl, stir occasionally, then let stand for 1 to 2 minutes.

3. Stir the gelatin into the warm cream and vigorously whisk until the gelatin and vanilla beans are completely mixed.

4. Remove from heat, and while stirring, pour mixture into ramekins and refrigerate for 3 to 4 hours before serving.

Raspberry Sauce

1. Follow instructions for Raspberry Sauce on page 230.

2. Pour raspberry sauce over each Panna Cotta.

Makes 8 to 10 servings

Sweet Lassi

Soothing and healthy, this is the perfect drink to enjoy with a curry especially if you are a fan, as we are, of curries made with hot curry powder.

Ingredients

½ teaspoon cumin powder

3 cups plain yogurt

2 cups ice water

⅓ cup superfine sugar

16 ice cubes

Directions

1. In a small, dry skillet toast the cumin on medium heat, stirring until it turns slightly darker (4 to 5 minutes).

2. In a blender combine yogurt, ice water, sugar, and cumin. Blend on high. Drop ice cubes into the blender, one at a time. Blend until smooth.

Makes 4 to 5 servings

<u>Notes</u>

Vegetarian Family Meal

Prayer at a Vegetarian Meal

Beloved and Holy Lord God,

You have blessed us with so many riches and so many choices. We offer our thankful prayer for this time of fellowship. We are reminded, Lord Jesus, of the meals where you were present while you lived and walked among your children. We know that you regarded those times at the table as times of fellowship and refreshment. We thank you for this food; may we never forget all we have here before us has been grown, cultivated, and prepared for our nourishment and our health. We ask that you guide and direct each of us to choose to live a life that brings honor, praise, and glory to you. Our Lord and Savior, Jesus Christ. Amen.

Prayer by Barbara Harris Youngflesh

Bible Verse

Praise the Lord, O my soul. O Lord my God, you are very great; you are clothed with splendor and majesty. . . . He waters the mountains from his upper chambers; the earth is satisfied by the fruit of his work. He makes grass grow for the cattle, and plants for man to cultivate—bringing forth food from the earth: wine that gladdens the heart of man, oil to makes his face shine, and bread that sustains his heart. (Psalm 104: 1, 13-15)

Menu

> French Onion Soup
> Saucy Avocados
> Lasagna with Red Bell Peppers
> Blueberry Crisp

French Onion Soup

Many years ago we enjoyed hearty bowls of onion soup late at night in the Les Halles section of Paris. Seeking a lighter soup, we switched from beef broth to chicken broth and finally to vegetable broth. This is the best!

Ingredients

1 tablespoon olive oil

3 tablespoons butter

5 cups peeled, thinly sliced onions

¼ teaspoon sugar

½ teaspoon salt

3 tablespoons flour

8 cups organic vegetable broth

⅔ cup dry white wine

¼ teaspoon freshly ground pepper

1 small loaf of French bread

1 ½ cups grated Swiss cheese (about 6 ounces)

Directions

1. In a large deep cooking pan, combine the oil and butter. Heat on medium heat until the butter melts, then add the onions. Cook the onions on medium heat, stirring frequently for 15 minutes.

2. Add the sugar, salt, and flour to the onions. Stir continuously for 3 minutes.

3. Add the vegetable broth and wine to the onions. Lower the heat (medium-low) and let the mixture cook for 30 minutes.

4. Cut the bread into slices 2 inches thick. Place a piece of bread in each soup bowl. Sprinkle the bread with the cheese. Pour the soup into the bowl and serve.

Makes 6 to 8 servings

Saucy Avocados

Growing up we loved any dish with avocados, as we always placed the seeds on the windowsill and watched them grow. In this fun combination, the sauce while warm is poured into the avocado half.

Ingredients

6 avocados

Ingredients for the Sauce

½ cup butter

½ cup tomato catsup

¾ cup chili sauce

½ cup sugar

3 tablespoons Worcestershire sauce

¼ teaspoon Tabasco sauce

⅛ teaspoon salt

⅛ teaspoon pepper

Directions

1. Cut each avocado in half but do not peel. Remove the seed.

2. In a saucepan, combine all of the ingredients for the sauce.

3. Cook, stirring, on medium heat until the butter is melted and the mixture is hot.

4. Pour hot sauce into the cavity of the cool avocado and serve.

Makes 12 servings

Lasagna with Red Bell Peppers

This winning combination is pretty and scrumptious. If fresh pasta sheets are not available, substitute dry ones and follow cooking instructions.

Ingredients

5 red bell peppers

2 to 3 tablespoons olive oil

1 pound fresh lasagna sheets

1 pound ricotta cheese

2 cups grated Parmesan cheese

1 ½ pounds fresh mozzarella, thinly sliced

1 cup pine nuts (Pignolias)

2 cups parsley, finely chopped

Directions

Preheat oven to 350 degrees.

1. Cut peppers in half and remove stem and seeds. Place peppers on a baking sheet (cut side down). Coat with 1 tablespoon of olive oil. Roast in the oven at 350 degrees for 40 minutes. Cool peppers and then peel. Chop one pepper into ¼-inch pieces for the garnish. Puree the remaining 4 peppers in an electric blender.

2. Drop the fresh pasta sheets into boiling water and cook for 1 minute. Immediately place the cooked pasta into cold water. Lay out. Pat dry.

3. Place pine nuts in a pie plate and bake in a 350-degree oven for 15 minutes. Stir occasionally.

4. Mix together the pepper puree and the ricotta.

5. Coat a 10 x 14 x 2 inch baking pan with 1 to 2 tablespoons olive oil. Place lasagna sheets to cover the bottom of the pan. Spread the ricotta, pepper puree, grated Parmesan, and mozzarella slices on top. Continue to layer lasagna sheets and toppings until pan is full.

6. Garnish with toasted pine nuts, parsley, and chopped red pepper.

7. Bake at 350 degrees for 25 minutes.

Makes 8 to 10 servings

Blueberry Crisp

Delicious with a scoop of vanilla ice cream or whipped cream.

Ingredients

4 cups blueberries

1 tablespoon lemon juice

⅓ cup sugar

Ingredients for the Topping

½ cup butter, melted

⅓ cup brown sugar, packed

⅓ cup flour

¾ cup quick cooking oats

Directions

Preheat oven to 350 degrees.

1. In a 2-quart baking dish, place the blueberries, lemon juice, and sugar. Stir gently to mix.

2. Combine the topping ingredients. Mix well. Spread over the blueberries.

3. Bake at 350 degrees for 35 minutes.

Makes 6 to 8 servings

About the Authors

Carolyn Anderson

Carolyn grew up in Indiana enjoying many days on her grandparent's working farm (which she now owns) surrounded by cooks, each competing to make the best home-cooked meal. Carolyn's mother and aunt were both home economics teachers. Carolyn holds BA and MS degrees from Boston University and Columbia University, respectively. She lives with her husband in Greenwich, Connecticut where she is president of her own real estate firm as well as past president of the Greenwich Association of Realtors. Her many interests include gardening, wine-making (she and her husband have had their own vineyard), and cooking. She attended Le Cordon Bleu's American course as well as many other cooking schools. She is a restaurant reviewer and the author of the ***Anderson Guide to Enjoying Greenwich***, published by Avocet Press (now in its 8th edition) with over 240 restaurant reviews. She is the author of ***The Complete Book of Homemade Ice Cream***, published in 1972 by Saturday Review Press and in 1974 by Bantam Books. It won awards and had an enormous number of favorable reviews, such as this 2002 review on Amazon.com: *"This is one of the best cookbooks I have seen. The exquisite detail and care put into the wording and detail of each recipe is incredible. I hope to one day see more by this author."*

Marty Harris Butler

Marty was planted and grew up on the same farm Carolyn visited. Driving a tractor, dealing with chickens, attending Hillisburg Church, and being in 4-H were part of her upbringing. Following graduation from Kirklin High School, she attended Indiana University, receiving BS and MS degrees. After teaching English and journalism at Frankfort High School for one year, she married her childhood sweetheart, Jerry, and together they produced four beautiful children. A successful twenty-year career in real estate in Kokomo, Indiana followed. She became a lay pastor in the Presbyterian Church and currently lives on the farm where Jerry was born and raised. Now a grandmother to seven wonderful grandchildren, her life is spent enjoying summer life in Culver on Lake Maxinkuckee and winters at West Bay Club in Estereo, Florida.

Tom Harris

Carolyn's cousin Tom, grew up on the family farm near Frankfort, Indiana where he helped his father farm. He still has fond memories of his childhood with his two sisters and two cousins. Life at that time was a blessing! He and his wife, Susan, currently live in Muncie, Indiana where they attend Westminster Presbyterian Church. Tom serves as an elder at Westminster and Susan and he sing in the choir. He teaches information systems courses in the Miller College of Business at Ball State University in Muncie. Susan and he have two sons who currently reside in Tulsa, Oklahoma.

Barbara Harris Youngflesh

Barbara's formative years were spent on the farm, where grandmother's house literally was 'through the woods!' It was a great childhood, and many treasured memories of family still bring a smile to her face and envy to her grandchildren! She has lived in six states (plus an 18 month stay in Switzerland) but now calls Houston home because her three sons and their families all live in Houston. Her career following graduation from Indiana University includes teaching home economics in Ohio, working in merchandising in Wyoming, and becoming involved with the International Quilt Festival which puts on the world's largest quilt show each fall in Houston. Friends and family keep Barbara young at heart and in spirit. She enjoys her close associations and activities at the Pines Presbyterian Church, P.E.O., and traveling with Quilts for their shows. Reading and simply spending time with her "grands" keeps her active and involved in living each day to the fullest.

Rosanna Anderson

Rosanna Anderson was born in the Midwest and grew up in university towns on both coasts. She is a pastor in the Presbyterian Church (USA) in her fourteenth year of ministry. She is married to Carolyn's son, Clifford, and enjoys raising their delightful son, Theodore. Family gatherings with Carolyn's delicious cooking and gracious hospitality are a true blessing and joy.

Vanessa Chow

Vanessa illustrated this book. She is a painter and sculptor of Hong Kong descent. Her newest paintings are inspired from her recent travels to Mongolia. She graduated from Connecticut College and has a Master of Fine Arts Degree in painting from The Rhode Island School of Design. She currently lives in sunny California where she enjoys surfing, making art and teaching art. She has exhibited her work in Los Angeles, New York, and Hong Kong. She has taught art in many places including Otis College of Art and Design, Mar Vista Elementary School, and the British American School. Vanessa is currently a faculty member of the Brentwood Art Center.

Real Family Life Menus and Recipes

My recipes are for dressy occasions as well as for family suppers. The recipes and menus are intended for active modern families. Some recipes are easy, others take more time. All of them fit the many moments in our lives. Not everyone grew up as I did, with a mother (Helen Hunt) and aunt (Wilma Harris) both teaching home economics. The menus help cooks decide what they might like to include in a traditional meal for Christmas or Easter or a Sunday supper. The recipes are a mix of favorite heirlooms and unique creations. On important holidays and family events, I want everyone to know how to put together a fabulous meal. I hope my menus and recipes will become their family favorites for future generations.

Real Family Life Prayers

My cousins' prayers are a way of giving thanks to God for life's blessings. Their prayers are in today's words, each one fitting the occasion and making it easy to give thanks before beginning a meal. These prayers are for everyone wishing to make prayer an ordinary part of daily life.

In my heart, I hope our book will inspire family traditions and values. Families cooking together and sharing meals together will have an opportunity as I did to learn life lessons at the dinner table. With parents working hard, our kitchen was a scene of family togetherness - me stirring, my brother setting the table, Dad mashing the potatoes, and Mom pulling it all together. As busy as we were, we always gathered around the table eating, talking, and growing up together. Families are returning to the table, and our book fits right into this trend.

Index of Recipes

Beverages

Breads

Breakfast

Desserts

Desserts

Raspberry Mousse —————————————————————————— 15

Red, White & Blue Indulgence ————————————————— 149

Sweet Potato Pie ———————————————————————— 222

Watermelon Sherbet ————————————————————— 34

Main Courses

All-American Spaghetti Pie ———————————————————— 46

Almond-Crusted Chicken Casserole ————————————— 142

Aunt Pearl's Chicken & Dumplings ——————————————— 192

Beef Rolls ——————————————————————————— 132

Beef Stroganoff ——————————————————————— 38

Chicken Curry ————————————————————————— 226

Chipped Beef Gravy ————————————————————— 80

Fish Baked in White Wine ——————————————————— 162

Herb-Crusted Roast Leg of Lamb ——————————————— 88

Holiday Ham with Raisin Sauce ———————————————— 64

Honey Peppered Salmon ——————————————————— 21

Honey Shrimp ————————————————————————— 101

Indiana Ham Loaf ——————————————————————— 110

Lasagna w/Red Bell Peppers ————————————————— 238

Lemon Tarragon Tuna ———————————————————— 174

Melanie's Chicken Satay ——————————————————— 102

Pepper-Crusted Steak ———————————————————— 10

Pizzas w/Many Toppings ——————————————————— 152

Sesame Scallops ——————————————————————— 100

Texas Chicken-Fried Steak & Gravy —————————————— 120

Texas Marinated Steak ———————————————————— 29

Turkey with Giblet Gravy & Stuffing —————————————— 212

Salads

Sandwiches

Sauces and Condiments

Almond Sauce ———————————————————— 168

Apple Butter ———————————————————— 70

Barbecue Sauce ———————————————————— 30

Hot Fudge Sauce ———————————————————— 155

Lemon Curd ———————————————————— 71

Lemon Mint Butter ———————————————————— 180

Mint Jelly ———————————————————— 87

Orange, Apricot, Peach Conserve ———————————— 148

Orange Glaze ———————————————————— 219

Peanut Coconut Sauce ———————————————— 103

Side Dishes

Applesauce ———————————————————— 135

Asparagus w/Lemon Dill Sauce ———————————— 22

Baked Beans Ora Hunt ———————————————— 32

Baked Potato ———————————————————— 81

Basmati Brown Rice w/Grapes ————————————— 104

Black-Eyed Peas & Rice ———————————————— 122

Brown & White Rice ———————————————— 39

Brussels Sprouts w/Pecans & Peppers ———————— 67

Carrot Casserole ———————————————————— 195

Cheese Ball with Carrots & Celery ————————— 48

Chestnut Stuffing ———————————————————— 214

Coconut Rice ———————————————————— 228

Corn & Beans in Nutmeg Butter ——————————— 40

Side Dishes

Corn Pudding ——————————————————— 215

Deviled Eggs ——————————————————— 91

Glazed Carrots with Fresh Mint ——————————— 112

Green Beans w/Herbs ———————————————— 194

Grits, Texas Style —————————————————— 60

Herb-Roasted Potatoes ————————————————— 90

Mashed Potatoes ——————————————————— 216

Peas in a Pod ———————————————————— 23

Potato Pancakes ——————————————————— 134

Potato Side Kicks —————————————————— 185

Red Cabbage & Apples —————————————————— 176

Rice with Fresh Herbs —————————————————— 161

Scalloped Oysters ——————————————————— 217

Scalloped Potatoes —————————————————— 113

Sweet Potatoes w/Coconut Topping ————————— 66

Sweet Potatoes w/Orange & Cinnamon ——————— 12

Soups

Apple Curry Soup —————————————————— 160

Borsch ————————————————————————— 130

French Onion Soup —————————————————— 236

Gazpacho ——————————————————————— 28

Grandmother's Chicken Soup ———————————— 184

Hot & Sour Soup ——————————————————— 172

Melon Soup ————————————————————— 20

Spinach Soup ———————————————————— 8

Notes